# MEMORY IMPROVEMENT

*The Memory Book to Improve and Increase Your Brain Power*

-

*Brain Food and Brain Health Habits to Enhance Your Memory, Remember More and Forget Less*

# EDOARDO
## ZELONI MAGELLI

# MEMORY IMPROVEMENT

© Copyright 2020 Edoardo Zeloni Magelli - All right reserved.

ISBN: 978-1-80111-963-4 - July 2020 - Original Version: Miglioramento della Memoria: Il Libro sulla Memoria per Incrementare la Potenza Cerebrale - Cibo e Sane Abitudini per il Cervello per Aumentare la Memoria, Ricordare di Più e Dimenticare di Meno (June 2020)

Author: Psychologist, Businessman and Consultant. Edoardo Zeloni Magelli, born in Prato in 1984. In 2010, soon after graduating in Psychology of Work and Organizations, he launched his first startup. As a Businessman he is CEO of Zeloni Corporation, a training company specialising in Business Applied Mental Sciences. His company is a reference point for anyone who wants to realize an idea or a project. As a scientist of the mind he is the father of Primordial Psychology and helps people to strengthen their minds in the shortest possible time. A music and sport-lover.

**UPGRADE YOUR MIND** → zelonimagelli.com

**UPGRADE YOUR BUSINESS** → zeloni.eu

The content contained within this book may not be reproduced, duplicated or transmitted without direct written permission from the author.

Under no circumstances will any blame or legal responsibility be held against the author, for any damages, reparation, or monetary loss due to the information contained within this book. Either directly or indirectly.

Legal Notice: This book is copyright protected. This book is only for personal use. You cannot amend, distribute, sell, use, quote or paraphrase any part, or the content within this book, without the consent of the author or publisher.

Disclaimer Notice: Please note the information contained within this document is for educational and entertainment purposes only. All effort has been executed to present accurate, up to date, and reliable, complete information. No warranties of any kind are declared or implied. Readers acknowledge that the author is not engaging in the rendering of legal, financial, medical or professional advice. The content within this book has been derived from various sources. Please consult a licensed professional before attempting any techniques outlined in this book.

By reading this document, the reader agrees that under no circumstances is the author responsible for any losses, direct or indirect, which are incurred as a result of the use of information contained within this document, including, but not limited to, — errors, omissions, or inaccuracies.

# CONTENTS

Introduction..................................................................9

## 1. How Memory Works......................................13

Biology..................................................................13

    Memory Models............................................16

    Sensory Memory............................................18

    Short-Term Memory.....................................19

    Long-Term Memory......................................22

    Brain Waves....................................................27

The Science of Learning................................32

## 2. Food and Lifestyle Choices............................35

Brain Food............................................................35

Lifestyle................................................................52

    Schedule Activities.......................................53

    Schedule Exercise.........................................55

    Sleep.................................................................56

    Monitor Stress...............................................57

    Practice Memory Boosting Activities......58

Monitor your Relationships...................................58

## 3. Interest and Memory....................................61

Observation..........................................................61

    Point of Focus..................................................63

    Imagination......................................................67

    The Brute Force Memorization Process.................70

    The Ridiculous Method to Remember Lists..........72

Leaving Home.......................................................77

    Building Links.................................................78

    Tips and Tricks................................................80

## 4. Numbers and Mnemonics.............................83

The Mnemonic Code..............................................84

    The Numeric Alphabet.....................................85

    Memorization...................................................92

    Association......................................................94

    Tips..................................................................95

## 5. Unlocking Keywords....................................97

The Gist of It........................................................97

    Memorizing Speeches......................................99

Creative Inspiration.................................................101

Applying the Method............................................104

## 6. Task Scheduling.............................................107

The Problem With Productivity...............................107

Multitasking.......................................................109

Dopamine Rush..................................................110

Your Brain and Multitasking...............................113

How to Work..........................................................118

Work Partitioning................................................119

Building a Routine..............................................123

## 7. Mind Mapping................................................131

Visual Imagery.......................................................131

What They Are....................................................133

Why Mind Maps Work.........................................138

Drawbacks..........................................................140

Aiding Memorization..............................................143

Tips and Tricks....................................................147

## 8. Tapping into the Subconscious Mind...........151

Mind and Brain......................................................152

- Conscious Mind .................................................... 154
- Subconscious Mind .............................................. 156
- Unconscious Mind ................................................ 163
- Training the Subconscious ..................................... 170
  - Meditation ......................................................... 171
  - Visualization ...................................................... 175
  - Affirmations ...................................................... 180
- A Better Memory, A Better You ................................ 183
- Bibliographical References ..................................... 195

"It's all about mastering yourself"


MARCUS TULLIUS CICERO

# Introduction

Our memory is one of those things we always think we need to improve but don't actually get around to doing anything about. This is quite tragic, in my opinion, because memory improvement is something that is easy to do and doesn't require any special abilities or superpowers. Yet, it is one of those things which when mastered resembles a superpower.

What are you willing to give up in order to attain a great memory? All of us are familiar with the saying 'in order to gain something one must give something up'. Usually, this conjures images of great sacrifice and a monk-like lifestyle. Well, in this case, all you need to give up is the price of this book and its predecessors in this series: *"Photographic Memory"* and *"Memory Training"*.

You will need to spend some time, of course. However, the good news is that you don't need to lock yourself in a room to specifically practice any of the techniques in this book. Well, you can if you want to but it isn't necessary. You can do all of them as you go about your day.

The best part of all this, as you will find out, is that an improved memory will benefit your ability to pick up a number of skills, aside from being a party conversation starter. Skills such as the ability to remember entire speeches, historical facts, learn foreign languages, sort out your daily tasks and so on. Last but not least, I'll also show you how an improved memory will improve your bottom line, that is put more cash into your wallet.

So what can you expect in the following pages? Can you turn into a memory supergiant? Well, that depends on you. The techniques do take work and a lot of people sabotage themselves by doing too much too soon. Take it slow and give your brain some time to adjust and catch up to things. You'll find that the adage 'slow and steady wins the race' very apt when it comes to training your memory. Remember that having a large memory is a skill. Like every other skill, you need to practice and exercise it. Think of your memory like a muscle that needs to be worked out. Exercise it too much and it exhausts itself and you risk an injury. Don't exercise it and it withers away.

Give yourself adequate rest and take it easy. You don't have to learn this stuff overnight. If you've practiced memory improvement techniques before, then you will be familiar with some of the ideas in this book. However, there are a number of more advanced techniques I will illustrate. Along the way, you will also learn how to adapt memory techniques to specific situations, all the way from using it to remember numbers, to learning a new language.

First of all though, it is important to understand the physiology of your brain. So without further ado, let's look at this first.

# 1. How Memory Works

We've always been led to believe that our memories are files which are stored inside a filing cabinet which is our brain. Another more modern description likens the brain to a supercomputer and the individual memories as files stored electronically. Given recent evidence though, the truth is that our brains and memories are even more complex and hard to understand through such metaphors.

Understanding the different types of memory and how our brain decides to store whatever it does is crucial for you to develop your memory skills.

## Biology

In simple biological terms, our memories are simply

a bunch of neurons firing together within our brains in order to recreate a past event. Thus, when we recall a previous event, our brain isn't retrieving some old file from its recesses but rather recreating the entire event by firing the neurons that were involved (Ifc.unam.mx, 2019).

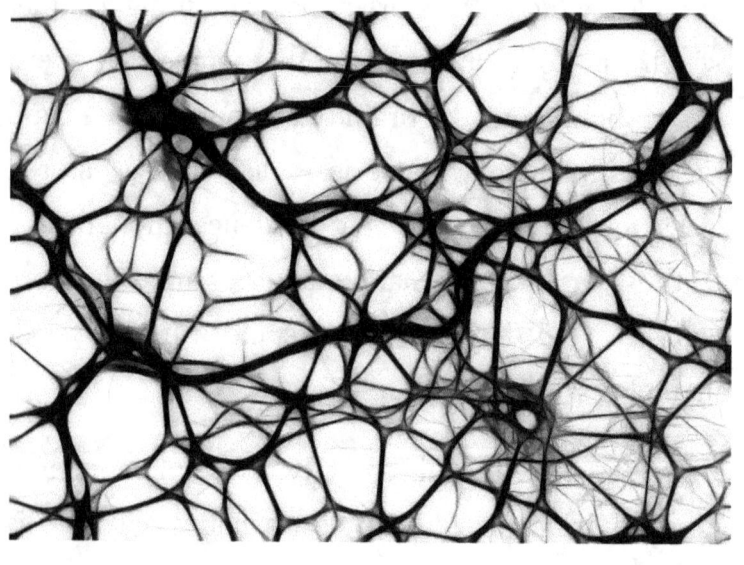

How does the brain remember which neurons fired at the time? Well, this is not fully known or understood. What is known is that the processes of memory and learning are linked. While learning involves the firing of new sets of neurons and building new neural pathways, memory recollection involves firing old ones.

The process of building new neural pathways necessarily requires the firing of the old ones and thus, we cannot learn without some form of memorization. We understand this instinctively. Take for example the case of learning a foreign language. In order to progress further and learn complex grammatical structures, it is necessary to memorize the letters of the alphabet and numbers first.

The temporal lobe within our brains is an important area with regards to our memories (Ifc.unam.mx, 2019). Damage to this portion impairs our ability to both learn as well as remember things. Jetlag and stress are some of the lifestyle factors that cause temporal lobe damage if unchecked, over a long period of time.

Our memories are not all the same. This is to say that there are different types of memories we store within us. Long-term memory is what we designate as 'memory' in everyday parlance.

## *Memory Models*

There are two popular models of memory which seek to explain how images and information are stored within us. One has a very rigid structure and is called the Atkinson-Shiffrin model, named after the scientists who proposed it (Human-memory.net, 2019). Under this model, memory is thought of as having three stages to it, sensory to short-term memory to long-term memory.

In other words, all information starts off as sensory memory, moves to short-term memory, before it is embedded into long-term memory. This model further breaks down long-term memory into stages. Long-term memory is divided into explicit or conscious memory and implicit or unconscious memory. Conscious memory is further subdivided into two more levels depending on whether we seek to remember tasks or facts.

Now, it isn't necessary for our purposes to dive deep into the model to understand it. Rather, it is to show how deep our memories go and really, how little we understand it. A cursory glance at this model will reveal that it doesn't take into account how subconscious memories are formed and how they influence conscious memories and decisions.

The second model tries to address this by removing all rigidity and simply explains learning and memory development as a flow from conscious to deep memory (Human-memory.net, 2019). This model is termed the levels of processing model and was proposed by scientists Fergus Craik and Robert Lockhart. The shortcomings of this model are evident by its inability to explain short term versus long-term memory, however.

Either way, we can conclude that there exist three types of memories: Sensory, short term and long term. So let's take a look at these in turn.

## *Sensory Memory*

This form of memory relates to retaining information received from our sensory inputs. Our impressions of the sensory inputs can be either ignored or acknowledged. When we acknowledge them, the information passes into sensory memory. The decision to ignore or acknowledge is the only conscious part of this memory, the rest of it functions automatically. This is how we can perceive things without touching them.

For example, if you see a steaming mug of coffee, you don't need to touch it to realize that it will be hot. This type of memory cannot be enhanced in any way via tactics such as rehearsal or conscious memorization, like memorizing a wall of text for example. The actual sensory memory lasts for less than a second before begin rejected or passing onto short-term memory.

The time it lasts is so short that it is often clubbed together with the perception process.

## *Short-Term Memory*

Short-term memory is often used interchangeably with the term working memory. This type of memory is what helps us complete tasks. For example, recalling earlier parts of sentences or conversations in order to continue them or finish a task. As the name suggests, short-term memory doesn't last for long and the information within is usually lost forever unless some effort is expended to remember it.

When an effort, such as repetition or other techniques, is put on memorizing the information, it usually passes into long-term memory instantaneously. There is some debate as to whether or not some form of editing or vetting takes place, especially when deep emotions are involved, but generally the transfer occurs quite quickly and there isn't much of a delay.

Working memory can hold from five to nine items within it at a time, according to various studies carried out (Human-memory.net, 2019). This may not sound like much but a lot of information that we store tends to be chunked. Chunking refers to a memorization process where a lot of similar information is clubbed together to memorize characteristics and qualities using a single word. For example, the word "car" is chunked into our brains to remember all its characteristics.

Similarly, the word "drive" is chunked into our brain as containing everything we need to do when driving. When learning to drive, our brain does not have any neural networks dedicated to this particular chunk of information and treats each task individually. Thus, the act of learning is really just teaching our brains to form more efficient umbrellas within which to place information.

The central executive portion of the prefrontal cortex is essential for short-term memory health. Studies have shown that damage to this area of the PFC results in short-term memory loss (Human-memory.net, 2019). Short-term memory, in terms of evolution, has played a very important role in the propagation of our species.

Our ability to focus and narrow down the most important things to work on and ignore or store other things for later, gives us a massive edge over other species. Thus, not only can we remember things for longer, we can also choose to think what we want. While this might seem impossible for those with overactive minds, with training, anything is possible.

Techniques to improve short-term memory including chunking and repetition. Repetition is simply hammering home the same information, over and over again. This is a particularly effective technique since the natural inclination of short-term memory is to decay and forget things after some time has passed, since it needs to make space for other, more pressing matters.

Thus repeating a piece of information to yourself will transfer it over to long-term memory and free up space within the working memory. Chunking, as explained before, is simply clubbing together similar concepts in order to absorb information better. It also refers to breaking up information that seems too complex. For example, a long number can be broken into smaller chunks and then absorbed in separate pieces.

Research shows that short-term memory can be made more efficient and information can be retained better into long-term memory by phonetically linking the sound associated with the information. Linking is a popular memorization technique, as explained in the first book of this series, and boosts short-term memory.

It bears to note at this point that boosting short-term memory doesn't mean you can hold more pieces of information within it. It's just that information flows into long-term memory faster and thus frees up additional space within working memory.

## Long-Term Memory

Long-term memory is what we think of when we speak of the topic but the reality is that this is the least understood of all the types of memory. Research has shown that long-term memory is just a collection of neural networks and the formation of a new memory is just a linking of existing neurons via connections, called synapses. The stronger and thicker the synapses are, the better we remember something.

However, synapses don't always disconnect or cease to exist. In some cases, especially extremely traumatic ones, synapses do tend to break and the memory gets lost forever but largely, this does not happen. This has led many researchers to question whether we ever really forget anything (Human-memory.net, 2019).

So how does one explain the fact that we cannot remember our infant days? Well, what happens is that old memories often get buried under a ton of newer, fresher neural networks and thus old memories get superimposed upon. Every once in a while, some trigger may occur which enables us to recall old memories and when this does happen, it throws us off for a few moments since our brain literally adjusted itself and this causes a feeling of disconnect for some time.

Speaking of triggers, while short term and sensory memory use the senses to remember and interpret things, long-term memory uses meaning and association. This is to say that things which are more important, as determined by our feelings, receive priority when it comes to storage and facilitate the lack of superimposition by other memories.

This is just a fancy way of saying that emotions matter when it comes to memorization. Connecting positive emotion to new bits of information is extremely helpful when it comes to storage. Long-term memory is further subdivided into conscious and unconscious or subconscious memory and we don't biologically understand how this works.

On a psychological level, we do know that our subconscious mind is just full of stuff that has passed from our conscious mind into it. These habits are old and ingrained and we perform them without thinking, like say the tying of a shoelace. However, what is the emotional impact of tying a shoelace? While we might have felt good when we first accomplished this as children, is that emotion really more positive than, say receiving love from someone we value?

So why does this memory pass into the subconscious and never get written over while many others comparable in nature don't? The answer is that we just don't know. Scientists posit that our brains might be prioritizing information received during the first five years and earlier years of our lives over the ones we receive when we're older, but there's no scientific proof to back this up (Human-memory.net, 2019).

From experience though, we do understand that children are learning machines and simply absorb everything around them unquestioningly, while old people tend to become cantankerous when their beliefs are questioned. In fairness, this applies to all adults, but the degree to which you can question a person's beliefs does decrease with age.

Biologically speaking, the prefrontal cortex and the hippocampus play important roles in long-term memory retrieval and formation. As we say with short-term memory, the way to push information into long-term storage is to simply associate it with adequate sensory inputs, think rhyming words and such, and then to imprint it into long-term memory, simply infuse positive and strong emotion into it.

Can negative emotion help? Well, yes, it can and the thing is that our brains are far more receptive to negative emotions than positive thanks to how we've evolved. From a psychological standpoint though, it should be obvious that positive emotion will do us a lot more good than negative emotion.

Positive emotions also affect our self-image. Again, we don't know how this collection of beliefs are stored but we do understand how to change them. Changing your view of yourself by changing your beliefs is very important.

There are methods that I often use with my clients, I empower their minds as quickly as possible by changing their limiting beliefs with empowering beliefs. But this is material for another book, and as such, I won't touch it here.

## *Brain Waves*

The communication between your neural networks via synapses are done via electricity. These electrical communications produce electromagnetic waves within the brain and based on the frequency of these waves, it is possible to detect what sort of states the brain is undergoing.

Now, before proceeding, I must warn you that there are a number of sources out there who assign magical properties to brain waves and their ability to change your life.

Claims such as increasing your IQ, improving your focus and so on by listening to sounds which are of the same frequency as the waves within the brain which produce the desired effect.

From a scientific perspective, none of these work (Novella, 2017). We will have to do further studies to understand if your brain is a tuning fork that can be induced to vibrate when it hears a sound and magically snap itself to attention. These solutions when they work, in most cases, are the result of the placebo effect. So music can alter our state of consciousness? Of course it can, think of your favorite relaxing music. Remember, any external stimulus can change your state of consciousness, even a word from a friend.

The information I'm presenting here is for knowledge purposes only and you should not take this as a method to increase your focus or memory.

Those techniques come later.

Briefly, the types of brain waves that exist are the following:

- **Infra low:** These vibrate at a frequency of less than 0.5 Hz and very little is known about what sort of activity produces them. Their low frequency makes it very difficult to detect and measure them.

- **Delta:** Delta waves oscillate between 0.5 to 4 Hz frequencies. These waves are produced when we're in deep sleep and are associated with healing since the body undergoes this process when we're asleep.

- **Theta:** Oscillating between 4 to 8 Hz, theta waves can be thought of as dream waves, correspond to a state of deep relaxation. When our minds are dreaming or in a subconscious state, between consciousness and unconsciousness, these waves are detected.

- **Alpha:** These waves are produced when we're fully present and peacefully focused on a task without any external distractions. So, a calm and concentrated mind. A calm state of consciousness. They oscillate between 8 to 12 Hz frequencies. In this state of mind we are more capable of storing and retrieving information.

- **Beta:** Beta waves are the most commonly present and occur during our normal day-to-day functions. For example, while you're reading this book, you're in Beta. It's an active state of consciousness. These oscillate between 12 to 35 Hz.

- **Gamma:** These are the waves of high performance. This is a favorite wavelength of the quacks. Maybe oscillating between 35 to

42 Hz (there's conflicting research), gamma waves are a bit of a mystery. Technically, they are beyond the spectrum of neuronal operation, but they do get produced when a person is in a state of great concentration, such as a great sporting performance or a delicate task that requires absolute concentration. It can also be a highly excited state, such as being in love. These have also been detected in people who have achieved a high level within their meditation practice. This has led to gamma waves being crowned the waves of spiritual enlightenment, which might be true, but don't be fooled, it's full of scammers and charlatans who play on people's weaknesses.

There are lively discussions among neuroscientists about brain waves, especially gamma waves. Therefore, pay attention to isochronic tones and binaural beats and the like, because they probably work mostly as placebos. There isn't a lot of scientific evidence backing up their efficacy. They certainly do not cause any harm if used sparingly. Like good relaxing music, sometimes they can give you a feeling of well-being. However, do not think of them as shortcuts to activate your brain somehow.

## The Science of Learning

This is a book on improving your memory, so talking about learning might seem tangential. However, as we've seen already, both processes share many similarities. Understanding, briefly, how to learn effectively will help you understand how to create deeper memory imprints, since you will have to learn new techniques.

Experiences are the best way of learning and a cursory look at our own lives will bear this out. Thus, creating a story of some sort prior to learning a new subject is an excellent technique. An example, in this case, would be to turn the learning of new memory improvement techniques into a quest of some sort.

This might sound childish, but perhaps, this is a good thing because children certainly know a lot more about learning than adults and seem to have more active imaginations than adults as well. Applying a sing-song tune to lists of words and associating new information with old are all techniques of applying new information to a storyboard.

Emotion is an excellent motivator to learn new information and opens our mind to new experiences. When in a deeply emotional state, our older neural networks are ripe for being overwritten and this is how undesirable habits, which are just networks, get overwritten. This technique of associating negative emotion with old habits and positive emotions with new ones is used for the purposes of recovery and rehab from drugs and alcohol (American Addiction Centers, 2019).

Focus and intentionality drive our learning to a specific goal. Focus helps you concentrate and intentionality is your "why", as in "why are you learning this?" The final piece of the puzzle is repetition. Doing a thing over and over hammers the neural network into shape and builds pathways.

Thus, with these four tools, focus, intentionality, emotion, and repetition, you can learn new information. There is no shortcut, you need to sit down and do the work.

So now having looked at the biology of the brain and the process of learning, let's take a look at how we can improve our ability to memorize and strengthen our brains via our lifestyle.

# 2. Food and Lifestyle Choices

The first step to improving your memory is to get your brain in as healthy a state as possible. While it might be impractical to fit a set of weights and lift them with your brain, your brain thankfully doesn't need such forms of exercise.

What it does need is for you to live as healthy a lifestyle as possible and in this chapter, I'm going to breakdown some of the factors that make up a healthy lifestyle.

## Brain Food

The brain is the command center of our bodies, making sure everything is in line and working to order. All in all, it's a big deal. The food you eat is the fuel that powers your body and brain and is also a big deal. These days, there's a lot of ruckus over what exactly is a healthy diet and the presence of chemically processed foods does nothing to answer this question.

The short answer is that a balanced and organic diet is the best form of food. There are some foods that some of us would rather not consume, such as vegans with regards to animal products. While this isn't ideal, it isn't a huge handicap either. As long as you get the right quantities of proteins, fats and carbohydrates along with vitamins and minerals, you'll be just fine and your brain will be in healthy shape.

Fat tends to get demonized quite a bit with a lot of people thinking it'll make them fat. Well, the reality is that fat is an essential macronutrient. What makes you fat is sugar, not fat (Kubala, 2019). Sugar is present in virtually every chemically processed food in the form of corn syrup and other chemicals, so this is the ingredient you should be staying away from.

Indulge yourself with some junk food if you feel like it but don't go overboard with it. I'd say the same thing applies to eating healthy as well. Our minds need some comfort food to stay healthy every once in a while so feel free to consume some unhealthy stuff once in a while to soothe your brain. Just don't overdo it.

There are some foods which will help your brain perform to its optimal state. Before we go down this list, understand that your brain will deteriorate with age. There is no food or drug you can take that will reverse the process. The best you should aim for is to be healthy and the best version of yourself.

**Fish**

Fatty fish or more specifically, omega-3 fatty acids, are the best brain food there is. Fish such as sardines, trout and salmon are rich in omega-3 fats. Your is mostly composed of water, but the rest is fat. The fats present in the brain are omega-3 fats as well and these are used to build neural synapses and networks (Jennings, 2017).

Studies conducted have shown that people who consume fatty fish regularly have a far lesser chance of contracting Alzheimer's disease along with benefiting from a number of other qualities of omega-3 fatty acids. These include younger looking skin, silkier hair and so on.

A deficiency of omega-3 has been linked to learning disabilities as well as mental states such as depression and anxiety (Jennings, 2017).

## Coffee

While consuming caffeine in large quantities can be detrimental to your health, an espresso after lunch is more than beneficial for you. It may help you in reducing sugar absorption. Also, caffeine increases your level of alertness, as any groggy night owl will attest. It does this by blocking adenosine which is a sleep-inducing chemical produced by the brain (Jennings, 2017).

Do not take coffee in the morning when you wake up, it is the worst time, because it is one of the moments in which our body releases more cortisol. You don't have to drink caffeine at a time when your cortisol concentration in the blood is at its peak. This is because cortisol production is strongly related to your level of alertness and it just so happens that cortisol peaks for your 24 hour rhythm between 8 and 9 AM on average (Debono et al., 2009). So it is advisable to take coffee when cortisol level in your blood has lowered.

Coffee also contains a number of antioxidants which help maintain overall cell health by destroying any free radicals within the body. A study conducted indicated that people who consume caffeine on a regular basis have a lower risk of contracting Alzheimer's disease and this might be due to the antioxidants present (Jennings, 2017).

However, you should get used to having coffee without sugar. If you can't drink it bitter, try adding some acacia honey. Don't drink more than one coffee a day. The quantity I would recommend is that of an espresso: 30 ml originating from 7 grams of ground and pressed coffee.

## Deeply Colored Berries

Blueberries, strawberries and raspberries contain a large number of antioxidants which flush toxins out of the body and reduce inflammation and oxidative damage within the cells (Jennings, 2017). A number of neurological diseases have been linked to the presence of free radicals and inflammation, thus berries are an excellent brain food.

Some studies conducted show that consumption of berries regularly can aid short-term memory as well (Jennings, 2017). This doesn't mean you start consuming bucketful's of blueberries every day but do make them a part of your diet.

## Turmeric

This spice has been used since ancient times for a number of things, from cleansing skin to as a natural sunscreen. However, one of the ingredients of turmeric, curcumin, is a substance that rarely manages to be absorbed directly by the brain. (Jennings, 2017).

Aside from being an excellent antioxidant and anti-inflammatory, curcumin helps boost memory and eases mental states such as depression (Jennings, 2017).

Consume this as part of your diet by adding turmeric spice to your food. This is usually present in curry powder, although you could just add turmeric directly. You can also add it to your tea, to orange juice or hot water with lemon and ginger.

The big limit of curcumin, however, is its poor absorption. In fact, a large part of the curcumin you consume is not assimilated and does not enter the blood.

**Broccoli**

Broccoli was widespread between ancient Rome and ancient Greece. This was thanks to the ancient Etruscans, a civilization dedicated to cultivation, who, thanks to their trade in the Mediterranean, spread this precious vegetable among civilizations.

These civilizations greatly appreciated the beneficial properties of broccoli, a precious food with extraordinary healing virtues. They are vegetables rich in vitamin C and mineral salts such as calcium, iron, phosphorus, potassium and zinc. They also contain vitamins B1, B2 and are an excellent source of vitamin K. This micronutrient is responsible for producing a type of fat which is extensively found in our brains (Jennings, 2017).

Studies conducted in elderly people show that those with higher intake of vitamin K have better memories and suffer from better mental health overall (Jennings, 2017). This is over and above it being anti-inflammatory and a potent antioxidant.

But the benefits of broccoli don't end there. They are high in fiber, have very few calories and a fair amount of protein. They are powerful antioxidants, have an anti-anemic, emollient, diuretic and purifying power. They protect bones and eyes, reducing the risk of cataracts. They help prevent cardiovascular disease and stroke. It's really an extraordinary food.

Broccoli contains very effective antioxidants: sulforane and isothiocyanates. In addition to preventing the growth of cancer cells, these substances also prevent the cell division process with the consequent apoptosis (cell death). So they have a protective action against tumors by limiting the development of cancer cells.

But sulforane has other beneficial properties, it helps the cells to cleanse themselves of toxins and is indicated against lung diseases. It has the ability to cleanse the lungs and mitigate inflammation of the respiratory tract.

We still have much to learn from ancient civilizations.

## Pumpkin Seeds

Zinc, magnesium, and copper are minerals that have excellent benefits for your brain. Nerve signals and memory are aided directly by these three minerals (Jennings, 2017). It bears to remember that the brain communicates via electrical impulses and these minerals happen to be highly conductive.

Pumpkin seeds contain all of these minerals in ample quantities and also contain iron which is essential for brain function and clarity. While the benefits are linked to the minerals themselves, pumpkin seeds are an excellent source of all of them and thus essential for a healthy brain.

**Dark Chocolate**

Chocolate is a mood booster as everyone knows. Milk chocolate usually contains a ton of sugars which do your health no good. Instead, dark chocolate and unrefined cocoa powder contain a number of plant fatty acids which aid brain function greatly (Jennings, 2017).

Thanks to cocoa, chocolate is one of the best food sources of flavonoids. They are natural substances that have antioxidant properties and repair cellular damage. There are various types of flavonoids, such as flavanols and flavonols, both of which are contained in cocoa.

Consuming a diet rich in flavonoids (in particular flavanols and flavonols) helps prevent type 2 diabetes (Zamora-Ros et al., 2013). In addition, cocoa flavanols may improve cardiometabolic health (Xiaochen et al., 2016).

These substances, are densely gathered in the areas of the brain which deal with learning and memory and studies have shown that people who consume dark chocolate tend to suffer less from degenerative brain diseases (Jennings, 2017).

**Nuts**

Nuts are great for your overall health, especially walnuts which have a good dose of omega-3 acids. The primary health effects of nuts seem to come from having a healthy heart as opposed to affecting the brain directly, but this is hardly a complaint (Jennings, 2017).

There have been studies linking heart and brain health and this should not come as a surprise given that these two organs form the nerve centers of our body (Jennings, 2017). In addition to this, nuts also contain healthy doses of vitamin E, antioxidants and prevent free radical damage at the cellular level.

## Oranges

The beneficial and nutritional properties of oranges are many. They contain fiber, minerals, vitamins and antioxidants, such as carotenoids, anthocyanins, citroflavonoids, flavanones, hesperidin and hydroxycinnamic acids. They are famous for their vitamin C content, although there are other foods that have more, such as grapes, currants, peppers, kiwis and broccoli.

Thanks to the presence of these beneficial substances, it is a precious fruit for our body, has anti-tumor properties and manages to increase our immune defenses. The presence of hesperidin present especially in albedo, the white of the orange, helps prevent cardiovascular disease.

But do oranges improve our brain? Do they help our memory? Yes. Orange juice is rich in flavonoids and improves cognitive function (Alharbi, Lamport et al., 2016). Our basic cognitive functions are attention, memory, perception and reasoning. Therefore, improving our cognitive functions means improving our process of acquiring knowledge and understanding through thought, the senses and experience. All this allows us to better store information.

The consumption of oranges also has effects on our mood. Sometimes even perfume can be enough to invigorate us and reduce anxiety. They are also good for our brain due to the presence of inositol, an important substance for our brain processes.

**Eggs**

The nutrients found within eggs, specifically vitamins B6, B12, choline and folate are excellent foods for the brain and improve mental cognition and memory. The body needs choline to synthesize phosphatidylcholine and sphingomyelin, two major phospholipids vital for cell membranes. Is an essential nutrient that must be included in your diet to maintain optimal health. Choline is also used for neurotransmission and regulates memory and mood.

Folate deficiency is detected in people with dementia and egg yolks are an excellent source of choline and folate (Jennings, 2017). Most people will have cholesterol concerns with consuming egg yolks, but as long as you exercise regularly and consume them in moderation, egg yolks are an excellent source of these micronutrients and protein.

Vitamin B6 is essential for the functioning of the central and peripheral nervous system and is essential for the synthesis of serotonin, which in addition to regulating our mood, is important for concentration and memory.

## Green Tea

Green tea (Camellia sinesis) is widely known for its anticancer and anti-inflammatory properties. It has been cultivated since ancient times and has been used for thousands of years by traditional Chinese medicine. Is an excellent source of antioxidants as well as amino acids which boost brain function.

On such amino acids, L-theanine increases the production of GABA ($\gamma$-aminobutyric acid), a neurotransmitter which reduces feelings of anxiety and induces calm (Jennings, 2017). This seems to balance the effects of caffeine in green tea.

Among the biologically active compounds contained in Camellia sinesis, the main antioxidant agents are catechins. The best source of these compounds is unfermented green tea (Musial, Kuban-Jankowska, Gorska-Ponikowska, 2020).

Of course, the antioxidant properties vary depending on the type and origin of green tea leaves. Geographical conditions, methods of harvesting and processing of leaves also influence. But basically, green tea leaves are rich in polyphenols and bioflavonoids. These antioxidants promote the regeneration of the tissues of our body and counteract free radicals and therefore help us slow down our cellular aging. They have a protective effect on neurons and reduce the risk of neurodegenerative diseases such as Alzheimer's and Parkinson's disease.

Catechins exhibit the strong property of neutralizing reactive oxygen (ROS) and nitrogen (RNS) species. They're the most widespread free radicals.

The group of green tea catechin derivatives includes: epicatechin, epigallocatechin, epicatechin gallate and epigallocatechin gallate. The last of these presents the most potent anti-inflammatory and anticancer potential. Notably, green tea catechins are widely described to be efficient in the prevention of lung cancer, breast cancer, esophageal cancer, stomach cancer, liver cancer and prostate cancer (Musial, Kuban-Jankowska, Gorska-Ponikowska, 2020).

# Lifestyle

You don't need to schedule separate times to conduct brain-boosting activities. The best way to do this is to actually integrate these within your daily life. The following tips will ensure that you can incorporate brain-boosting activities as part of your daily routine.

You will not begin to follow all these tips right away most likely. No matter, this is no need for concern. When looking to incorporate change, always make sure to do so in small steps. This goes back to the neural conditioning of our brains.

Older neural networks are quite strong and if you seek to implement new habits, what you're trying to do is to overpower these old, strong networks with new, weak ones. You might be able to temporarily achieve some dominance but eventually, your strength will run out and you'll go back to doing the same old thing.

This is why new year resolutions fail because people seek to change their lives drastically as soon as the year begins. Within a few weeks or months, they're back to doing the same old thing. The way to avoid this situation is to gradually establish the new neural network's strength, step by step.

Thus, you don't need to expend your willpower trying to force yourself to do something new. Bite-sized steps are the answer, always remember that.

## *Schedule Activities*

Our brains love activities which give it a great workout. The best way to give it a workout is to incorporate the following elements:

- **Novelty:** something new that the brain doesn't know is a great way to refresh your mind. Doing something old in our routine, but in a new way is also a great way to incorporate novelty into your life. For example, driving a new route to work.

- **Challenge:** an activity that requires constant engagement is perfect for the brain. While the level of challenge can vary, it is important that the brain doesn't go into autopilot. For example, playing a new video game level that requires you to reason your way through as opposed to replaying a challenging level which you've already cleared.

- **Learning:** pick activities that have a learning curve. This is an excellent way to ensure that the challenge remains. Plus, you'll actually learn a skill.

- **Reward:** if this activity gives you some tangible benefit in your life, this will motivate you to stick to it for longer.

Examples of activities that incorporate all of the

above are learning new hobbies, learning to play music, learning a new language and so on. Constantly giving your brain a workout keeps it sharp.

## *Schedule Exercise*

You don't need to go out and build a mountain of muscle on yourself but just move and break a sweat. This not only releases endorphins into your system and benefits your heart, but it rids your brain of toxins. Exercise also has huge benefits by combating depression and other mental states that result from frustration. Picking a physical activity like swimming as a hobby is an excellent way to combine the previous point about novelty into this.

## *Sleep*

Our toxic work cultures somehow think that it is a sign of strength to work on little sleep or pull all-nighters. Sure, there are some instances where this is required but doing this repeatedly is just madness. Sleep is essential for your body to heal and repair itself, especially if you're physically active. Sleep helps your brain to remember whatever it has learned and rid itself of toxins. An average adult needs around eight hours of sleep every twenty-four hours.

I have been using "Zeloni Magelli's Rule 888" for years. Eight hours of rest, eight hours of work, and eight hours of pleasures, passions and fun. Try it too!

Make sure you prioritize sleep by making sure your bedroom is properly dark and there aren't any loud noises around. If need be, play some relaxing music or nature sounds to help you sleep better. A top tip is to avoid staring at a bright screen an hour before bed. This includes things like television or a smartphone screen. I also advise you to protect your eyes with sunglasses when using your PC, tablet and smartphone. It may seem strange, but your sight will thank you.

Keep the phone off and in another room when you sleep. And don't turn it on right away when you wake up in the morning. First have breakfast, read, dedicate yourself to your most important thing. After you have done all this, you can turn it on and open up to others, but not before! You have to protect your mind and your spaces.

## *Monitor Stress*

Following the previous steps will alone ensure that your stress levels will remain low. However, stress inducers exist everywhere and you should monitor yourself for such symptoms. Often stress is caused thanks to unrealistic expectations on our part and streaks of perfectionism.

Make sure you monitor yourself for these types of behavior and take steps to release the stress. Meditation and yoga are excellent methods to handle stress. Schedule some fun activities to carry out. Go to the spa and book yourself a massage. Reward yourself well and stop being so harsh on yourself all the time.

## *Practice Memory Boosting Activities*

Alright, this one's a bit self-serving but nonetheless, memory boosting activities incorporate novelty and provide a fresh challenge for you. Plus, they work your brain out directly. Learning other learning techniques, studying mnemonics and playing brain-boosting games are excellent ways to keep yourself entertained and boost your brain health.

## *Monitor your Relationships*

Our relationships are the biggest sources of stress and pleasure, often at the same time. Make sure your relationships are healthy and always be proactive when it comes to managing them. Too often we take them and the people involved for granted and let things slip.

There is a lot of stigma, unfortunately, still associated with seeking help when it comes to repairing a relationship. Do not be afraid of seeking out and addressing problems and always make sure your relationships are a source of strength and not something that debilitate you.

This brings to an end our look at a lifestyle that supports and boosts brain health, memory being one of them. You've thus far learned about the biology underlying the brain as well as how your lifestyle affects its health.

Now it's time to dive in and look at specific exercises and specific situations where an excellent memory will benefit you.

# 3. Interest and Memory

In this chapter, my aim is to prove to you that there is no such thing as a bad memory. No, I'm not talking about a nightmare you had recently, I'm referring to your belief that you forget things easily or find it difficult to remember things and have to write everything down.

As we've already seen, your brain doesn't forget things (except short-term memory). Things get superimposed upon, but forgetting? No, this doesn't happen since neural connections do not break, except in very remote conditions. The starting point of all memory is interest and observation, as we'll see.

## Observation

You're walking down the road and as you pass by a shop window, you see a massive display advertising a product, say a beard trimmer, which catches your eye. You don't have the time right now to go in and purchase it but file it away for later. As you go about your work day, you remember the display and can recall all the information it contained about the product.

If you happen to be a beard trimming enthusiast, or are looking to buy something as a gift for a male, you might even discuss this product with some of the people around you. You might not have the time to physically go to the store and purchase it but you manage to order it online and have it delivered to your home shortly thereafter.

So, what magic took place that caused you to remember that object? Why did you even notice the product as you passed it by? We're bombarded with a lot of advertising imagery these days and are inured to most of it, to the extent that our brains have begun to blank out most of these ads as we scroll through a webpage. I mean, when was the last time you didn't skip a social network ad that gave you the option?

Here's another exercise for you. Do not write anything down as you read through this and work on everything mentally: Let's say you're driving a public bus. At the first stop, four people enter and two get off. At the next stop, no one gets on but two exit the bus. At the next three stops, three people each enter the bus and two exit, except for the last stop where only one exits. Following this, at the next four stops, one person enters each, except for the last stop where three people enter. At each of these four stops, one person exits.

Got all that? Right. Now, my question to you is: what is the name of the bus driver?

## *Point of Focus*

The above is a game that some school children play with one another and even if you've never played this before, you can appreciate my point here. You see, your focus was probably on the numbers and as you kept reading you probably tried to work out the sums and keep track of the number of people on the bus.

If I'd asked you at the end how many people were remaining on the bus, you'd have had a ready answer for me. This is because once I started rattling off the numbers, your interest was piqued by it. By interest, I don't mean to say I stirred deep passions for numbers within you, just that I got you to focus on them.

However, I asked you the name of the bus driver at the end, which is not something you were interested in or focused upon. Those of you who have already encountered this exercise previously may have the answer ready. Well, for such people here's a follow-up question: How many stops did the bus make? Didn't keep track of that, did you?

This exercise deals more with observation than memory, but the starting point of all memory is observation and interest. You only observe things you're interested in. Therefore, in order to work on training your memory, you need to first have an interest in doing so. You need to inject positive emotion into it, as we saw in the previous chapters.

If you do this, your brain has a great incentive to work with you instead of against you. Right now, if you've convinced yourself that you have a poor memory, your dominant neural network with regards to this belief compels you to write everything down. If you suddenly stop writing things down, without generating an interest in training your memory skills, you're not going to go anywhere and will soon regress.

Interest goes beyond wanting to develop your memory skills. You also need to be interested in what it is you wish to remember. Now, I'm using the word interest here for lack of a better expression, in the latter case. Perhaps memorable is a better word. Your interest is piqued by things which have some emotional meaning for you. The deeper the emotion is, the more likely you'll remember it and react to it.

Let's say you're faced with a choice of deciding which advertisement would work better for a surface and floor cleaner. One ad shows a video of a rat scurrying around and generally creating a racket, ruining everything it touches. The second ad shows a cute puppy running around and doing puppy things and ends with it looking at the mess it has created and saying 'sorry' in a cute voice over. I mean, the choice is obvious, isn't it? Unless you're that exceptional person that happens to love rats, everyone is going to pick the puppy. Why is this? Again, you probably understand this instinctively and I don't need to explain this. The net result is that you're going to remember, memorize in other words, the product better when you see the puppy instead of the rat.

In short, the puppy created a more memorable and interesting experience for you to remember. But to tell the truth, you would also remember advertising with the rat, because it is unusual. And therefore it would equally attract your attention. But it would be a bad choice for the product. We also remember not only positive emotions, but also negative ones.

## *Imagination*

We have vivid imaginations, this is without a doubt. You only have to think of the disaster scenarios that some people regularly visualize in their heads to understand that our brains are capable of some truly outstanding feats of cinema making once the shackles of reality are loosened.

You probably remember some memorable dreams of yours and a few nightmares as well perhaps. This shows that when it comes to memory, your brain does not distinguish between real and imaginary. Every experience is treated equally and stored within. This is why visualization as a technique to improve yourself is so powerful.

If you visualize scenarios where you are successful in a task or even in life generally, your brain will recall and remember these moments and inject you with confidence. The key is to fuse positive emotion into these experiences and make them as real as possible. The deeper the better.

Imagination and memory are connected. As we bring memories back to mind, a process that reshapes our memories and perceptions occurs on an unconscious level.

Our imagination overlaps and intertwines with our memory. We cannot imagine something without the basis of a memory of our past experiences. And we can't remember without using our imagination.

The point is that imagination is a powerful tool when used consciously. Imagination can make things memorable and get us to focus on the things we wish to remember.

Even your imagination can be considered as a muscle that needs exercise to be trained. Regular visualization exercises will help you train yourself and will indirectly boost your ability to remember things.

A good visualization exercise is to dream up scenarios such as a perfect day or a perfect week. Extend it to a perfect life if you want.

When you first do this, your images will be hazy and you'll have trouble making them real. Keep at it though, and you'll soon find that you'll be able to visualize things for one hour easily. While all of this visualization is well and good, how does it help your memory? Is there an exercise you can do to use imagination to aid your memory? Of course, and it's a method that can replace the brute force memorization process.

## *The Brute Force Memorization Process*

Although the name may sound new to you, it is the method you used most often at school to store information. For example, endlessly repeating a poem until you have memorized it. But this method is not very safe and effective. Think of all the poems you have memorized in the past. How many do you remember today?

How can you improve this technique? I use my method which I called *"Augmented Brute Force"*.

Imagine having to memorize a poem. Get pen and paper. Read the first line of the poem you want to learn and write it 3 times on the sheet of paper. Read the second line and write it 3 times. Keep going until you reach the last line of the poem. Are you done? Now you'll have the whole poem written where each line has been repeated 3 times. I want to give you a visual example, on your sheet of paper you will read:

Line 1,

Line 1,

Line 1,

Line 2,

Line 2,

Line 2,

and so on...

Once finished, you will have to repeat everything for 2 more times. You will end up with 3 written poems where each line has been repeated 3 times. These 3 "augmented" poems will now have to be read aloud. And you will have to record an audio. Then you will have to lie down on the bed with your eyes closed and listen to this audio 3 times. When you get up, you will have learned poem by heart.

Why is this method very powerful? Because it is a

concentrate of techniques that work together and amplify your ability to remember.

You will use repetition, writing, reading aloud, listening and alpha waves of your brain. When you lie down and close your eyes, you will enter a state of calm and your brainwaves will be alpha type. As we have seen before, these waves favour learning and memorization.

In addition, in this process, you will stimulate 3 of your 5 senses: Sight, Hearing and Touch. This is a technique with a very high memorization power. Augmented Brute Force! Try it!

But now back to the imagination. How can we memorize without using traditional brute force? How can we use the imagination to help our memory? Here's a method.

## *The Ridiculous Method to Remember Lists*

Milk, chicken, water, cereal, whole wheat pasta, brown rice, carrots, celery, oatmeal bread, majorero cheese, eggs and Marseille soap. Try to memorize that list and see how you go. Probably tedious, right? It requires some mental effort and brute force memorization. I mean, as we saw before, repeat it until you memorized it. This is probably how you used to remember things in school and unfortunately, most of the people haven't learned a better way. Well, I'm about to give you the perfectly ridiculous method to remember lists. You'll understand why it is called so shortly. It is a set of some techniques that we have already discussed in previous books in this series.

Given what you've learned thus far in this chapter, it should be obvious that our first step to remembering this list is to make it as interesting and memorable as possible. There's nothing inherently interesting about a grocery shopping list, which is what this is. So what do we do? Well, this is where our imaginations come in!

What are some of the most memorable experiences in our lives? Probably trips. We loved them as children and as adults, we invest money and set aside special weeks to take them. A lot of memorable occasions are followed or preceded by trips. So why not take a trip?

The key to this exercise is to take a trip through a place you know like the back of your hand since you want to focus on remembering the list and not the place you're traveling through. Your home is the perfect place for this. Since it's your home, it's not going to excite you very much, but this is where the ridiculous portion comes in.

As you travel through your home, from the living room to the dining room and so on, you need to place the objects in that list along the way and exaggerate their qualities to such an extent that you cannot possibly forget them. For example, you open your front door and the first thing you notice is a sea of milk rushing over you or a life-sized gallon jug of milk asking you if you remembered to buy the milk.

Then, as you turn to go into your bedroom to get changed, you see a fire breathing chicken demanding a glass of water, right now, damn it! As you open the door to your bedroom, there's a cereal box lying in your bed snoring loudly and laughing hysterically because it's dreaming of something funny.

You get the idea. Take your time and make these images as ridiculous and funny as possible. Don't let any constraints of reality hobble your vision and walk throughout your home, placing these oddities wherever you please. At first, you'll have problems concentrating on the particular areas of your house and placing objects.

Start off slow. Instead of placing the entire list, place a few objects and write down the rest. Then slowly increase the number of objects you place. Remember to make the trip through your house as sensible as possible. So don't jump from the front yard to the upstairs bedroom. The idea is to make the objects memorable, not the trip itself. The trip should be an automatic and sensible response.

As you place the objects, don't name them but remember their qualities. Thus, don't call the judgmental milk bottle "milk" but simply notice what it is and move on. When you wish to recall the first item on your list, simply take the trip again and you'll encounter it. Thus, you'll remember milk, then chicken and so on.

A good idea is to make these images funny. Humor is an extremely positive emotion and is something we're naturally attracted to. I mean, you could turn these images horrifying as well since those can be memorable too but, do you really want to? Besides, if you associate negative emotions such as fear and shock with memory exercises, chances are you won't follow up on them regularly.

As you become more proficient with this, you'll be able to zoom through your home and remember everything on your list. It is at this point that you should take things up a notch and challenge yourself. Remember, your brain loves challenges, no matter how much it complains. It is crucial for you to keep throwing new challenges at it and exercising it.

# Leaving Home

If you find that after some time you're able to run through or fly through with great speed through your home in your head and are able to easily place and thus remember lists of ten items, take things up a notch by practicing the linking method and leaving the confines of your home.

Linking refers to associating one object with another. Studies have shown that we tend to remember things which remind us of something else. Thus, we remember and associate water with a pool or sand with a beach or an emotion with a particular time of our lives.

You can use this psychological tactic to remember longer lists and recall items on this list with greater speed than the ridiculous method which requires you to travel through your home or a familiar place. Linking is something you should take bite-sized pieces of at first since it will place a greater cognitive load on you.

However, remember that any new exercise will be tough at first and you need to keep practicing in order to get better at it.

## *Building Links*

Using the previous example of our grocery list, your task is to build links between each successive item on the list. For example, the first item, milk, needs to be linked to the second, chicken. Again, it is important that you make the link as ridiculous as possible for reasons already explained.

A chicken swimming in milk isn't ridiculous enough, unfortunately. How about a chicken chugging a bottle of milk and burping loudly, throwing it on the floor demanding "More" like a cowboy in a western movie? After this, the chicken rubs its tummy and begins to burp out cereal into a large box. I am aware that what I wrote in these lines is not very elegant. But I'm also sure that this image has remained more impressed on you than a chicken swimming in milk. You were able to visualize it better and it surprised you. So you will be able to remember it well. I'm sure you understand the real meaning of "ridiculous" now.

Linking method is really just a more advanced form of the ridiculous method where you still take a journey but down your list instead of placing items in a familiar spot. By severing your reliance on the familiarity of your surroundings, you're placing greater trust on your brain's ability to rely on just the pictures on the list and associate the items with one another, instead of associating the item with a familiar place.

The key to building strong links is to make the picture as ridiculous as possible but don't spend too much time making it ridiculous. The first picture that pops into your head is usually the most powerful and don't worry if you think it isn't ridiculous enough. Change the picture only if you find that you can't remember it upon review.

## *Tips and Tricks*

There are some techniques you can use to build better links. The first of these is sizing. Simply put, this means making the items either very small or very large. Gigantism has a more profound effect on us and we tend to rate things bigger than us as more memorable than those tinier.

Making something heart-wrenchingly cute is also a good tactic. There are very few people in the world who wouldn't smile at a puppy or a baby and this is simply our natural desire for expressing love shining through. The positive emotions this generates makes the image memorable enough to stick with us for a long time. If you find giant puppies cute, then go for it.

Giving dynamism and action to your items is another good idea. Have them do ridiculous things while moving around and don't leave them static. The idea of movement is again something that generates positive associations in our mind. This is why we journey through our home and our list, since the implied movement refreshes our brain and brings it novelty.

When dynamism and movement are associated with an external object, we still feel the same emotion thanks to the strength of the mental associations with movement. So use it with your images. Other good tactics, which I've already mentioned, are humor and exaggeration. We love laughing and our sense of humor is something a lot of ourselves identify as a cornerstone of our identity.

A tactic that works for some is substitution. This involves performing an activity with an item on your list that would be ridiculous to do in real life. For example, trying to hit a baseball with a compass. The principle that underpins the effectiveness of this method is still its absurdity.

Try to incorporate more than one technique into your visions and keep practicing and building your skills. Remember that a skill is something that develops via repetition, focus, intentionality and emotion. Use these principles to build your memory, which is but a skill. This brings to a close our look at the role of observation and interest with regard to memory. Remember the key is to generate interest, preferably positive, in your lists or objects to memorize and your brain will do the rest for you.

By the way, the bus driver is you. Did you forget the question? Did you really think I would forget to give you the answer?

# 4. Numbers and Mnemonics

While it is easy to memorize and travel through lists of words, numbers pose a particular problem. Numbers are merely shapes we've memorized and unless they are connected to a special memory, they don't have too much meaning for us.

Complicating the problem is the fact that there are so many combinations. There are ten base numbers but these ten combine to form an infinite number of combinations which makes it seem impossible to remember things.

In this chapter, I'll give you a foolproof method to remember any number, no matter the size using a method which will build on the previous methods we've looked at thus far.

# The Mnemonic Code

The idea of using mnemonics to memorize something is hardly groundbreaking. It was also known in ancient Greece. In fact, "mnēmonikós" derives from Mnemosyne, the Greek goddess of memory. Mnemotechnics was very important in ancient times, even before literacy, because knowledge and cultural traditions were handed down orally.

Some mnemonics, as we saw in the first book *Photographic Memory*, rely on the use of sounds to correlate them to words or to shorten complex phrases in a sound that makes sense.

A good method for remember numbers is to assign a letter or sound to each base number, from zero to nine, and to thus create sounds for a number or set of numbers. However, this method breaks down when dealing with large numbers since there will be many sounds to memorize.

Further complicating the issue is the fact that none of these sounds will mean much to you and it will become difficult for you to memorize them. Thus, instead of memorizing numbers, you're now memorizing sounds and the link back to the number which is a pretty roundabout way of doing things.

Well, I'm going to show you a method that will help you use mnemonics the right way and enable you to memorize long lists of eight or nine numbers easily. The key is to utilize our old friends, imagination and linking once we move past mnemonics.

## *The Numeric Alphabet*

The first step is to create your own alphabet for the numbers from zero to nine. The mind processes images. Therefore a complex number must be displayed as a set of images. To transform numbers into images we need a code. Everyone has their own methods of doing this and I'm going to explain mine below.

**0** - O. Zero looks like an O so this makes sense to me.

**1** - A. A is the first letter of the English alphabet.

**2** - B. The second letter.

**3** - C. The third.

**4** - D. The fourth.

**5** - E. The fifth.

**6** - S. I think of six starting with an S so this makes sense.

**7** - L. The symbol 7 may look like an inverted L.

**8** - H. The number 8 on a digital clock display can remind an H.

**9** - N. Nove comincia con la N.


You need to come up with an alphabet that makes the most sense to you instead of trying to memorize the one above. The key is to use associations and links that make the most sense and are almost intuitive for you. For example, I find it natural to associate the letter E with the number five. Some of you might not find it so.

The key is to suspend logic and use emotion instead. Remember, emotion is one of the main drivers of memory and you need to use it in your favor. When you think of a number, what is the first thing that pops into your mind? Well, use the associated letter with that number. You might think of the word "run" with "one" for example. So use the letter "R" or some such association to denote that letter.

You need to memorize this new alphabet before proceeding. The next step is to assign some character to two-digit numbers. By assigning them personalities and actions, you can bring them to life and it becomes pretty easy for you to make linkages. Fair warning, this method is brutally effective, but it will seem tedious at first.

What I mean by assigning a personality to two-digit numbers is best illustrated via an example. Let's take the number 67. The letters corresponding to this are S and L. So 67 is SL. The next step is to assign a personality and an action to SL. By personality, I mean a famous person or some piece of pop culture which will immediately get you to associate with it.

Personally, SL evokes the images of SNL to me so I think of it as Saturday Night Live (a comedy show that's been on since 1975) and the action I associate with it the most is laughter. Since exaggeration is a good thing, I'm going to exaggerate this action by turning laughter into guffawing, while holding my sides, or an image of a person holding their sides laughing uncontrollably which causes me to laugh as well, thanks to laughter's infectious nature.

So we now have the following:

67 = SL = SNL and laughing uncontrollably

As further examples let's take the number 99. This corresponds to NN which, to me, evokes the images of a "deep night", then I think of a superhero punches a villain in the face. To further clarify, I visualize the Batman comic strips where he punches villains with the words "bam" and "biff" in explosive little clouds, colored red and yellow.

You can use whatever you want to signify the letters and actions. The key is that they should have some impact on you and you should be able to instantly recognize and denote the action and the pop culture personality. Keep it short and simple and like I said, you'll find that the first thing that pops into your head will be the most memorable. It should have caught on by now that you're effectively using your existing memory to build new ones.

Since your existing memories have been implanted thanks to emotions, it makes sense to use these existing ones instead of trying to conjure new emotional connections by extending the associations.

These associations you make to the numbers don't need to make sense. If you choose associations thinking they'll sound cool to someone else, you're going about it all wrong. They're your own business, so keep them to yourself.

Sometimes, your associations will not be politically correct. This isn't about judging yourself or censoring yourself in any way. If you are troubled by some associations, work on deactivating the beliefs that propagate the connection, instead of trying to pick something that has a secondary impact on you.

A good exercise to free your mind and really open your imagination is to write out a list of numbers from 00 to 99 and ascribe references to them along with an action. For example:

**00** → OO → Two large eyes that express amazement.

**01** → OA → Sounds like Aloha. So Hawaii. Hawaiian flower necklace.

**02** → OB → Reminds me OBI, the DIY retailer. I think of the wooden gazebo that my father built.

**03** → OC → Orange County, California and surfing, sunset on the beach, bonfire on the beach (in this case my action is a collective one which signifies a certain mood. As long as it makes sense to you, go with it)

**08** → OH → Shocked emoji and a person going "ooooh"

**45** → DE → Germany and driving fast on the autobahn.

**38** → CH → Switzerland, wooden houses in the mountains and hiking.

**58** → EH → Ed Helms and a dentist pulling out a tooth

**46** → DS → MS-DOS and typing away at a computer

Write out an entire list, as many numbers as you can, from 00 to 99 and let your mind give you images and actions. Remember to simply pick the first thing that comes to your mind. Sometimes, this will not make sense, especially when you first do this. However, stick with it and release your mind, you'll find yourself having a lot of fun with it.

## *Memorization*

Now that you're able to automatically associate references and actions with numbers, it's time to start using this to help you memorize long numbers. We're going to use our old friend chunking here to help us assimilate the information we need to memorize.

If we have a long string of numbers, like a telephone number, say 6142099456, we first need to break this number down into two-digit chunks. So 6142099456 turns into 61, 42, 09, 94 and 56.

61 → SA → South Africa and playing cricket.

42 → DB → Deutsche bank and stealing money.

09 → ON → Robin Hood and Archery.

94 → ND → Notre Dame and the hunchback of Notre Dame dancing a jig.

56 → ES → Spain and bullfighting.

Now that you have your list of references and actions, it's time to weave a ridiculous story by alternating between the reference and the action. Thus, 6142099456 becomes South Africa stealing a ton of money from Robin Hood because the hunchback of Notre Dame wants to party in Spain and needs the dough.

I understand that this seems like an extremely tedious exercise to do and you're probably thinking there's no way you'll ever be able to remember the steps or the associations. Well, trust me, after a few tries, you'll be able to fly through this. This brings me to the final step of the process. While it's great to build a story and this associate it with a number, it doesn't help you in cases where you need to associate the number with a name. For example, you know the number is 6142099456, but whose number is it?

## *Association*

The final step is to create a link between your story and the subject. So if you're trying to memorize a friend's phone number, set the story in their home or a location associated with them. Location is just one method of association. You could also have some element in the story remain constant that you associate with the person you know. For example, you could have the subjects of your story wear a particular item of clothing that you associate with your friend. Or perhaps these subjects hold something belonging to your friend. And so on; the choices are endless.

By forming an association to such a bizarre and nonsensical story, you're pretty much guaranteeing that your brain will remember the number. As always, the more ridiculous your story is, the better. Now this will be heavy work at first. You will require some time to create a story and also form associations and actions for the numbers involved.

However, once you keep practicing, you will find yourself getting better at it and eventually, you'll be able to instantly come up with stories and actions and memorize long lists of numbers. You won't need to keep saving phone numbers or write them down anywhere, you'll be able to recite them off the top of your head.

## *Tips*

Using mnemonic code are all about creating memorable stories. Right from the very beginning when choosing your own alphabet for the ten base digits, you need to come up with something that strikes you immediately and with emotion. Again, as mentioned in the previous chapter, the first thing that strikes you is usually the best choice.

The same applies to the second step where you need to associate the two-digit numbers with references that you understand along with actions that seem plausible for those subjects. Don't pick random actions which don't make sense but don't go off the deep end trying to get things to make too much sense either.

Lastly, practice. Practice a lot. This technique will be a lot easier once you master the material in the previous chapter since your brain will be trained to a certain extent by then. Don't be frustrated or give in easily. Remember that over time, you'll be able to apply this technique effortlessly.

This brings to a close our look at memorizing number lists and associating them with people they're connected to. Next, we'll look at something which brings out a cold sweat for most people: public speeches.

# 5. Unlocking Keywords

Public speaking is one of those things that is at the top of most people's fears. Public speaking brings about such fear that memorizing a speech or utilizing memory in any manner seems impossible thanks to the nervousness it spawns.

Well, in this chapter I'm going to give you a shortcut to mastering public speaking. This will be done using the very sort of hyperactivity your brain undergoes during moments of strain.

## The Gist of It

Public speaking is just one of the many occasions where the keyword technique is useful. Other places you can use this is when memorizing a lot of facts, such as during a history lesson involving a lot of dates. You can use the method in the previous chapter to remember these and then link the date to the keywords you will choose for the fact blocks.

Keywords will also help you learn the meanings of phrases in foreign languages a lot faster. However, truth be told, its use in learning the entirety of a foreign language is a bit limited and most of the time, the best way to learn a new language is to immerse yourself in it and communicate with it as much as possible. Listening and brute force repetition, in other words.

The keyword technique is also not useful for long-term memorization, unless you explicitly make that your goal. The technique itself helps short-term memory, and I'm using this term here as different from working memory which can hold just seven facts at a time, on average. By short term, I mean something that you'll remember for a week or two and then forget unless you keep repeating the information to yourself.

Remember that I'm only using public speaking as an example to illustrate how this works since this is one of those extreme situations that works well to show you the benefits and pitfalls of the technique. This method is by no means confined to just memorizing speeches.

## *Memorizing Speeches*

When confronted with a large crowd the first thing that disappears is our focus. To combat this, a lot of people try to memorize their entire speech, but this is actually the worst way possible of dealing with the fear of public speaking. This method is not very effective, since it causes your brain to focus on what comes next and in effect, what the speaker has does is create a link between every single word in the speech.

Thus, as one word comes out, the entire tsunami of words come tumbling out. All this works right until a link breaks and the person forgets a word. That is the moment when the speaker fumbles and stammers and the crowd begins to get antsy as well. Not to mention the fact that a person who memorizes an entire speech can hardly be expected to deliver it in an engaging way. In such cases, the speaker's mind is so focused on the minutiae that they forget the larger purpose of the speech, which is to entertain the crowd and get them invested with the topic.

The best public speakers do not bother with memorizing their speeches and neither do they write out their speeches word for word. Instead, they let the moment carry them away and draw inspiration from it. For example, did you know that the words "I have a dream" do not appear anywhere on Dr. Martin Luther King's notes prior to him delivering that seminal speech? He made it up in the moment (Grant, 2016)! The part that made history was improvised. A spontaneous speech is stronger than a prepared speech.

The method that was used by Dr. King and numerous other accomplished public speakers is keywording. Basically, this involves breaking down chunks of information into summaries and then picking a word or a phrase that embodies the idea they wish to speak about.

Next, by linking the different keywords together, the speech receives its framework or outline and the speaker is free to color in what's missing. This is a particularly effective technique because it fully utilizes our brain's internal capacity to remember and to be creative.

## *Creative Inspiration*

Creativity refers to something that pops out of existence that wasn't there before. To create is to produce from nothing, even if in reality a transformation of something happens.

Why does the painter choose to paint this spot black and that spot yellow? No one knows, maybe not even him. All he knows is that it "feels" right. Hearing musicians speak, all one hears is how the moment moves them to produce music.

I played for many years with my band, my guitar solos were always improvised, they always changed, I was inspired by the moment. It was like I was connecting to something above me, and my fingers were moving by themselves.

Creativity is not something that arises out of memory and as such, memorization doesn't have much to do with it, on the surface at least. However, examining the conditions that inspire creativity is instructive since it appears that good memorization can create these conditions.

Think about the last time you did something creative. Your brain was probably at rest and relaxed. You were not burdened with day-to-day tensions and had not probably given the matter a lot of conscious thought. Problem-solving occurs when our brains are at rest, oddly enough, not when they're hyperactive.

Going back to the public speaking example, if you happen to know the course or journey your speech ought to take, you'll be far more relaxed.

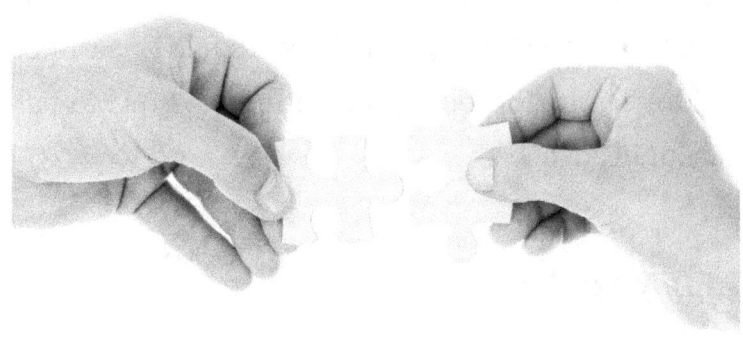

Firstly, you don't need to remember every single word from your speech since you only need to remember your keywords or your gist words.

By linking these together what you've done is you've established a story which can easily be recalled and recounted without much effort. This leaves your brain free of worry to focus on making things better.

This way, a flow is established and your brain gets to exercise its creative muscles since it can find inspiration in the moment and convey the information with the right emotional impact and depth.

The biggest fear people have with regards to public speaking is making a fool of themselves by forgetting what to say or saying something stupid. This can be addressed by thoroughly preparing the topic to talk about in advance.

## *Applying the Method*

Implementing the method is pretty straightforward. If this is the first time you're doing this, it's a good idea to write your speech out in advance, word for word, and then review it. Remember, you don't need to memorize the whole thing, just review it to see whether it makes sense to you or not.

Next, identify the transition points within your speech. Transition points refer to areas where you switch from one topic to another. Mark the end of one topic and the beginning of another. Now, you'll have broken down your speech into chunks of topics.

Once this is done, read through the individual chunks and write down a phrase or an idea that best encapsulates what it is you're trying to communicate within that chunk. You could use a word but for first timers, I recommend a phrase since this will be easier to remember and construct a story around. As you become more proficient, you can use a word.

The final step is something that should be familiar to you. Link all the phrases together by forming a story, as ridiculous as possible, to weave a common thread through all of them and commit this to memory. Repeat the story to yourself repeatedly in order to do this and when the time comes for you to speak, start with the first link and you'll find that your brain will supply the correct words.

The key in all of this is to trust your brain. Remember that your brain is more than capable of memorizing and remembering things by itself. It's just that there's a lot of other rubbish that gets superimposed upon it and hobbles its natural behavior. So trust and have faith in your brain and carry this out. You'll find yourself a wonderful public speaker.

While speaking in public is great and everything, our work lives are an extremely important part of our day-to-day activities. Given the amount of time we spend at work, it is a good idea to review and look at how memory plays an important role and how you can boost work performance via a few simple adjustments.

# 6. Task Scheduling

As we've seen before the first key to memory is attention. If your attention has external demands being placed upon it, there's very little chance you're going to be able to finish your current task properly. Think of it this way: You might think you sent that important email to your client, but the reality is that it's still sitting in your drafts folder waiting to be sent.

Why has it gotten harder to focus at work and get things done? In this chapter, I'm going to break down this topic and give you the key to getting things done in half the time by using your inherent memory skill.

## The Problem With Productivity

The internet is a wonderful thing and has brought the world closer together. But it also gave rise to some bad habits. For some reason, for many employees, the best way to guarantee that sweet year-end bonus is to send emails at three in the morning.

This has led to a bizarre belief that the more things you can do at once, or juggle, the better you are as a worker. What was previously the dominion of circus performers has now become the go to strategy for every white-collar worker out there and anyone who doesn't oblige or live up to this standard is looked down upon.

The problem with remaining connected to work all the time is that it actually decreases productivity. Sure, it's useful to remain connected in case of an emergency but it's no coincidence that the number of emergencies at work seem to have spiked since all this connectivity came into being. So what's really going on here?

## *Multitasking*

Juggling has been given a more business friendly and managerial makeover by calling it multitasking since the turn of the millennium. This is when you answer emails, while on an important call and also issue commands to those working for you in order to get things done quickly. Some people are actually dumb enough to think this is a good thing.

The fact is, our brains are not designed to work this way. Research conducted at Stanford University shows that people who multitask are actually less productive than those who don't and are significantly worse at switching off from a certain task and switching to another one (TalentSmart, 2019). Their quality of work is, as a result, far less than those who refuse to multitask.

What's worse is that multitasking actually reduces your productivity over time. Biologically, this makes sense since you're weakening your brain steadily over time and can hardly expect it to be able to keep up. By staying constantly connected to work or engaging in work related thoughts all the while, you're never switching off and giving your brain a moment to relax and absorb what is going on.

The net result is a low quality of work that only increases the number of things you need to get done, the exact opposite of what was the primary objective. Yet, people continue to multitask. Why is this? A part of the reason is inertia. We simply do not change unless given a powerful incentive. Think of it as Newton's first law.

A uniform rectilinear motion will continue indefinitely in the absence of friction or any other external force. An object in motion will remain in motion until an external force is applied to it. This is how we work as well. A bigger reason is biological and has to do with the way our brains work.

### *Dopamine Rush*

So how do you schedule your tasks? If you're like most people, you probably create a to-do list, which you now know how to memorize, and then work your way through it. The to-do list is an excellent productivity tool and condenses everything into one place. Even better is that its reward system is built-in. There's something very satisfying when crossing something off your list.

This is where the problem begins, however. Once you cross things off, it feels good because you receive a rush of dopamine, which can be thought of as the 'feel good' hormone (Newsonen, 2014). It is a hormone responsible for the sense of gratification, it is a catecholamine, like adrenaline and norepinephrine, so there is also a right charge and energy to continue to finish the list.

Since dopamine is involved in promoting behaviour and stabilising habits, this hormone motivates us to take action. The more dopamine that is released from a particular activity, the stronger that particular neural pathway becomes. After all, this is just emotion embedding a habit or memory deeper into your brain.

Thus, we begin to chase that good feeling and seek to cross things off our lists faster and faster. This leads us to do as many things as we can at once, reasoning that the more things we can get done, the quicker we can cross things off. The result of all this warped thinking is doing three things at once and boasting about your multitasking abilities on your resume.

The dopamine rush warps our judgment in many ways. Not only do we produce a lesser quality of work, we also lose our ability to prioritize things. What happens over time is that we start filling out lists with nonsensical things, and we turn into paper shufflers. These tasks are mundane and ridiculously small and amount to shuffling a few papers on your desk.

The real goal of your task is forgotten and as a result, you end up becoming a paper shuffler at work. Even worse, there's other stuff going on in the background which you don't realize.

Even if crossing some things off your list makes you feel good, those things don't have to go on your list!

Let me tell you about the Principle of Pareto. The principle states that about 20% of causes create 80% of effects. So, 80% of what we get is caused by only 20% of what we do. In every field or sector, most of the effects are caused by a limited number of causes.

So, if most of the results come from a small part of our actions, it means that most of what we do is of little value and is quite useless.

From now on, just focus on the 20% that generates 80% of your results! Give up the rest and delegate it to other people. In addition to improving your productivity, you will improve your life.

### *Your Brain and Multitasking*

The most astonishing study, which demonstrates how useless multitasking, is been conducted at the University of London (TalentSmart, 2019). In this study, subjects were ordered to multitask a variety of complicated goals. These goals were things which occur regularly in a workplace such as sending an email when engaged on a call and so on.

The findings showed the when multitasking, the average IQ of the subjects decreased dramatically, almost as much as if they had imbibed drugs or alcohol. Not just a small quantity, mind you, but as if they'd stayed up drinking all night.

Even more damning was the finding that their average IQs dipped to the level of an eight-year-old. In effect, when you're trying to send an important email while doing something else or are engaged elsewhere, you might as well let an eight-year-old write it for all the good you're doing.

IQ is a misunderstood metric and doesn't signify the overall intelligence of a person. In fact, the person who originally proposed the score intended for it to be used as a metric to gauge the potential of a child who scored low on the scale, indicating a gap in the education process (TalentSmart, 2019). Over time, this has been misunderstood to mean a marker of overall intelligence.

IQ increases and decreases according to the environment we're in. If you're in an unfamiliar place where no one speaks a language you understand, your effective IQ is going to be about the same as a bunch of bricks, notwithstanding that Ph.D. from MIT in your back pocket. IQ can be thought of as the measure of cognitive stress on your brain currently. The more relaxed your mind is, the better you work and the more intelligent you are.

Aside from lowering your IQ in the moment drastically, even more worrisome is that constant multitasking actually damages your brain. Previously, research had postulated that the damage that occurs from multitasking might be temporary but new studies conducted at the University of Sussex indicates that the damage might be permanent (TalentSmart, 2019).

Researchers found that those who regularly multitasked had less brain density in the anterior cingulate cortex. This portion of the brain is responsible for another extremely important factor when it comes to evaluating our intelligence, our emotional quotient or EQ.

EQ tends to take a bit of a backseat to IQ since it cannot be measured via a number but is instead observed. Simply put, EQ is a measure of how "with it" you are in a situation. Laughing out loud at a funeral or weeping tears of sadness at your best friend's baby shower are extreme examples of a close to non-existent EQ.

While it might not be measured, EQ determines the quality of our lives in a number of ways. Aside from helping or hampering our relationships, it also determines how well we do at work. Studies have shown that high level executives possess high EQ levels (TalentSmart, 2019). Thus, the implication is clear and truth be told, it is something all of us innately know. To do well in life, one needs to get along with those around us.

Has this suddenly turned into a book on productivity? No, not really. The point I'm trying to get across here is that your memory is a deeply innate quality and is something that needs to be taken care of. It all starts with how well you look after your brain. This is why I spent a good chunk of time giving you a list of brain food and addressing lifestyle factors.

The truth is that our brains have the ability to remember things extremely well. Remember that the brain cannot forget things, biologically speaking. Things do get overwritten but the original information is all there inside. It's just a question of revealing them and bringing it back up to the surface.

Take care of your brain. The long-term damage that is caused by constant multitasking only weakens you and is far more harmful than the short-term gain you receive from the dopamine rush of crossing things off your list.

So how are you supposed to work? Is there a handy framework which you can follow to get things done better and take care of your brain at the same time? Of course! Let's find out together.

## How to Work

There are a number of working strategies out there but picking the one that is the best for your brain's health is a daunting task. Well, the easiest way to reduce the noise is to simply go back to what we've learned thus far. Our brains can only handle one task at a time and thus your work strategy is simple: do one thing at a time!

This strategy goes by a lot of names called deep

work, monotasking, single tasking and so on. Let's break down the elements of this a bit more.

## *Work Partitioning*

It's easy enough to say that you should do one thing at a time but practically speaking, this is a daunting task. Thus enters the solution of partitioning. Setting aside time specifically to complete important single tasks versus the time spent doing multiple paper shuffling tasks. It all starts with your priorities, of course.

You need to classify your task lists on the basis of most to least important. A good framework to follow here is the famous Eisenhower method which classifies tasks in the basis of a matrix. The factors involved are urgent and not urgent on the horizontal axis and important and not important on the vertical.

What is important has a high impact on what we do, what is not important has a low impact.

|  | URGENT | NOT URGENT |
|---|---|---|
| IMPORTANT | Now!<br>Do it now! | Schedule<br>Schedule a time to do it |
| NOT IMPORTANT | Delegate<br>Who can do it for you? | Delete |

*Figure 1: The Eisenhower Matrix*

Thus, the tasks to focus on deeply are the ones which are urgent and important rather than not urgent and not important. Once you make your list in this fashion, it will become quite obvious which ones need to be monotasked. At first, this will be a difficult thing to do. You might be accustomed to simply throwing things out on paper and listing them in no particular order and on getting things crossed off. This method requires you to pause and really think about the things you need to get done. So take the time and make a conscious effort at first. This activity has the added benefit of giving you an idea of the framework within which the task needs to be completed.

Once your list is done, you need to pick a partition framework. In his book, *Deep Work*, Cal Newport mentions four frameworks which you can use to partition your tasks (Newport, 2016):

- **Monastic philosophy:** deep focus on your tasks all the time.

- **Bimodal philosophy:** split time into chunks of months, weeks or a year to focus on important tasks and spend the rest of the time doing the less important ones.

- **Rhythmic philosophy:** divide your day between focused and multitasked work.

- **Journalistic philosophy:** Do focused work whenever your schedule allows it.

As you can see, each approach has its own pros and cons. The monastic philosophy is aptly named because you'll end up in seclusion most of the time and your default response to anything other than your work will be a "no". The bimodal philosophy is easier to work with if you can afford it.

I really like to take months and weeks off to focus on just one task. I regularly schedule time to seclude myself in nature and to work and meditate on a particular task that is important to me.

The rhythmic philosophy is what most people will land upon. For example, using the early hours of the day to tackle the most important task, restricting meetings and e-mail to a few hours in the afternoon. Spending the time in an undisturbed state of focused work is the best way to get things done at a high level of quality.

Don't underestimate the early hours of the day, they can determine how your life turns out.

The last philosophy is an opportunistic one and might not work for some. For example, if a meeting gets canceled you can use that time to focus deeply on a task. But it seems that most people would use this time for multitasking rather than extending their already scheduled periods of focused monotasking.

## *Building a Routine*

When starting off with monotasking, it is important to take small bites at it, like with everything else. Schedule small windows of focused work and build your capacity. One of the beautiful things of focused work is that you'll find fifteen minutes of highly focused output will be equivalent to an hour's worth of usual work, if you're an avid multitasker.

Thus, begin with small windows of twenty-five minutes and take a refreshing break of however long you need. I mention however long because at first, you might need half an hour or more to recover. I don't mean to say recover from damage or anything of the sort but the fact that your brain will need to adjust to the new routine. Once it gets accustomed to it, you'll be able to get by with five to ten-minute recovery breaks after half an hour or an hour of focused work.

Your location for monotasked work is extremely important. The advice the Newport gives in his book is to switch up the locations every so often because it gives your brain a dose of novelty (Adegbuyi, 2019). As we've seen, novelty keeps the brain fresh and changing your environment is one of the best ways to do this. Perhaps you find the office too dreary? Look to convince your boss if you can work from the conference room instead, or a cafe if you're really adventurous.

Set a fixed routine during this time. For example, you will drink just water and not caffeine and will not answer and even check your phone for messages. Naturally, all forms of internet and social media should be avoided religiously. Schedule your breaks meticulously too. Do not check anything with regards to work and don't focus on the problem at hand. The rest period is actually where the magic happens and your brain's subconscious mechanism gets working. The creative impulse works in the background and you'll often find that when you consciously return to work, you'll have ideas as to how to solve the issue at hand.

One of the things you must do is to eliminate tasks which do not add enough benefit to your life. Unfortunately, there are people who tend to perform tasks from a perspective of missing out on them. For example, they check social media often because they worry that they'll miss out on some important update from a loved one. They check the news every so often because they're afraid they might miss out on some important news items affecting their lives.

Here's the thing: if something important enough to affect our lives does take place, we'll know about it. Your family member isn't going to keep you out of the loop in case something happens and the effects of world news will be felt by you soon enough. Work towards cutting these poisonous things out of your life entirely instead of restricting it to your rest periods.

Studies have shown that the news and popular social media works to enhance our negativity bias (Adegbuyi, 2019). This is another way of saying that it makes you more likely to look at the miserable side of things than the positive and you don't need any help in that regard, to begin with.

You have to know that staying exposed to bad news won't help your mental health. You could react in two ways. The first is to activate a defense mechanism to maintain your balance, starting to feel indifference, detachment and loss of empathy. The second is to absorb negativity, developing anxiety, depression, insecurity, uncertainty about the future, panic attacks and fear.

Often, those who listen to bad news start complaining. Surely, complaining is never the solution. Complaints are harmful, both the ones we create and the ones we suffer. They have a negative effect on our neurons and the functioning of our brain. They serve to make you discharge your negative and hidden emotional states of mind that are to the detriment of those who suffer the passive effect.

Complaints activate cortisol, the stress hormone, which has negative effects on the hippocampus, which is the brain region that participates in the processes of memory, learning and imagination. This shuts down your problem-solving skills and also affects your future choices.

Stay away from complaints and don't complain. You're going to create a reality in your subconscious exactly the same as the complaints you hear or create. So get away from it all.

Try to create a routine without exposure to negativity and without complaints. Complaining is just a waste of time and energy that prevents your brain from developing new ideas and solutions. The last things I would like to mention are to schedule time to read and think. Who's your most valuable client? It's you. Sell yourself at least an hour a day. You must take time to improve yourself.

It's important to think about the opportunity cost of this hour. On one hand, you can check social networks, read some online news, and reply to a few emails while pretending to finish the memo that is supposed to be the focus of your attention. On the other hand, you can dedicate the time to improving yourself. In the short term, you're better off with the dopamine-laced rush of email and social networks while multitasking. In the long term, the investment in learning something new and improving yourself goes further (Farnam Street, 2019).

Benjamin Franklin once said, "An investment in knowledge pays the best interest." He knew the value of constantly becoming more knowledgeable. In fact, just about every successful person in the world has one thing in common: they are constantly reading and educating themselves on a daily basis (Bryant, 2016).

*"Develop into a lifelong self-learner through voracious reading; cultivate curiosity and strive to become a little wiser every day."*

Charlie Munger

Read to learn new information and then think about it. Sit quietly in a room and think about things in your life. Focus on the things important to you and what you would like to accomplish.

Thinking deeply and in a focused manner is simply a form of meditation and gives your brain a good workout. You don't need to spend hours on end doing this, even fifteen minutes is enough. You'll find yourself refreshed mentally and keen to get back to the task at hand. Don't make the mistake of scheduling this activity during your break time though.

Focused thinking requires work and effort so it's best to set it aside to either earlier in the day, soon after you wake up or before you go to bed at night.

Our brains are extremely conducive to new ideas at these points in time so make full use of it.

> *"Go to bed smarter than when you woke up."*
>
> Charlie Munger

Practicing focused work, via monotasking, will keep your brain healthy and primed to absorb more information. In other words, it'll help you function better and memory is one of the things that will improve thanks to this.

# 7. Mind Mapping

Often used as a productivity tool, mind maps are nonetheless a fantastic way to remember complex ideas and tasks. The simplicity of the technique is what makes it powerful. In addition to showing you how to create mind maps and how they boost your productivity, I'll also be showing you how to create maps that remain in memory, so that you don't even need to refer back to the paper they were created on.

## Visual Imagery

While every person learns in a different manner, each and every one of us responds well to visual imagery. Either as a video or a picture, images can transform the learning and memorization process. If you think back to your most cherished memories the way you recall them are through striking images that stayed with you and the emotions they engendered.

While generating emotions for mind maps is a bit of a challenge, you can take advantage of their visual element and use this to enhance your ability to remember things. Mind maps are often used as an organizing tool and to breakdown complex ideas and tasks. For example, at the start of a new project at work, the project manager will often create a mind map to help visualize the various problems that need to be addressed and the issues that will crop up.

Mind maps also breakdown abstract ideas and thoughts and make them more concrete simply by forcing them to be jotted down on paper. Writing is an extremely powerful learning tool and is remembered by our brains a lot faster than typing or any other form of recording information (Wax, 2019). The best way to learn something as quickly as possible is to infuse emotion into the information and then write it down.

Although I have already dealt with mind maps in the first book of this series, I think it would be appropriate to go into more detail. So let's take some time to better understand what they are and how they can be used.

## *What They Are*

Mind maps are visual tools which are created by a person instead of a linear list of ideas. The idea of the mind map was first proposed by the British psychologist Tony Buzan in his book *How to Mind Map* (Buzan and Buzan, 1996). Buzan, in his book, proposed that creating imagery related to the task at hand made more sense than creating a linear list since most problems are complex and iterative in nature.

This is to say that a lot of problems don't follow a step-by-step solution path and instead you will need to revisit earlier steps and redo them even if you haven't made a mistake. This scenario is always encountered at the start of a new task where there isn't a clear path forward and the path has to be created instead.

Thinking iteratively, that is creating a process which takes into account revisiting older steps, is difficult if you make a list. A list forces our minds into a linear thought pattern and thus reduces the overall vision. Moreover, Buzan proposed, it shut us away from our creative minds (1996).

This information has been proven wrong since. But Buzan's theory was that linear thinking forced us to use our analytical abilities and thus engaged just the left half of your prefrontal cortex, which was thought to be the side of the brain responsible for organizing things and analytical ability. The right-hand side, by comparison, was the one which was creative and was probably a hippie given the way studies proposed its qualities (Buzan and Buzan, 1996).

Buzan proposed that by creating visual imagery you got to engage both your creative right and the analytical left with regards to your problem and thus attacked it in novel ways. While his left and right hemisphere theory has been proved wrong since, Buzan's ideas actually hold up very well nonetheless (Buzan and Buzan, 1996).

Recent studies show that the dichotomous distinction between "right hemisphere" and "left hemisphere", despite its validity, appears a little too simplistic, incomplete and imprecise (Lucarelli, 2015).

It is not easy to describe what happens in our brain when we think, when we process sensory stimuli, when we plan or perform motor activities; we know, however, that many areas of the different lobes (frontal, parietal, temporal and occipital) are involved in both hemispheres (Lucarelli, 2015).

The brain doesn't work in hemispheric isolation but rather as a team. There is no doubt however, that if you apply analytical processes to a task, you're going to be engaging analytical thought patterns within you and thus, the creative side will be suppressed a bit. The mind map removes this obstacle between the processes.

Mind maps are drawn by hand on a piece of paper with the problem to be solved at the center. You can think of it as being something like in Figure 2.

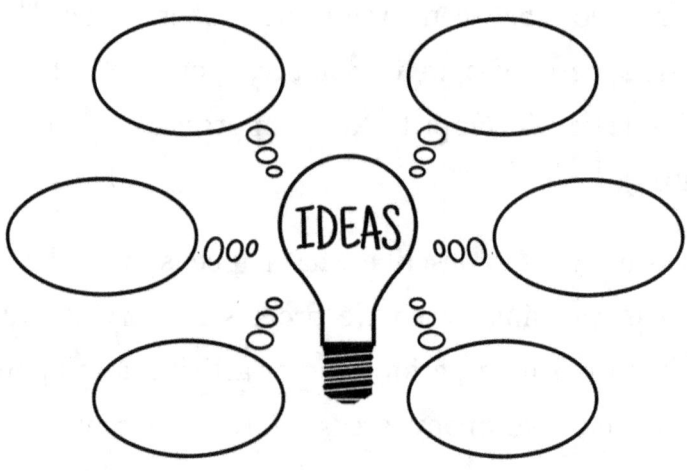

*Figure 2: An Example of a Mind Map*

In Figure 2, the bulb in the center contains the word "ideas" but you could substitute it for your problem at hand. You don't need to draw a lightbulb in case you're wondering. Simply draw a circle and write the gist of your problem, or your keyword, in the center and then make connections to other thought bubbles. You can have as many thought bubbles as you want. You can have connections from the central idea to the bubbles and between the bubbles themselves. The idea is to be as expansive as possible. Solutions to problems don't come to us in a linear way and the mind map removes the issue of how to order them. Once a mind map is created, it becomes a lot easier to reduce that into an ordered list.

Given its visual nature, it's also very easy to designate something as being more important than anything else or to fix a relative order of priority.

The strength of the connection between the central thought and the bubble signifies the importance. In other words, simply draw a thicker line to the more important ideas and thinner as they decrease in order of priority. Use different colored pens if necessary; the choice is entirely up to you. It's your map after all!

## *Why Mind Maps Work*

To understand why mind maps work so well, we need to revisit our old friends, chunking and association. Remember that your brain likes taking in information one chunk at a time, instead of a whole gulp of it and it remembers better when the information entering it is associated with something it already knows.

Not only does it remember better, but it understands the new concept better. Understanding plays a huge factor in memorizing a memory because rote learning, or brute force memorization, can only take you so far. This is a good example of the distinction between short-term memory and long-term memory. Recall that we learned earlier in this book that short-term memory depends on sensory input to remember whereas long-term memory is emotive and associative.

Memorization is a part of the learning process. Thus, simply hearing the same words again and again will only help you remember things for a short while, whereas understanding it by associating it to some existing information will enable you to truly learn it.

We can surmise that this associative method of thinking is radiant in nature. In other words, it is not linear and it spreads out in multiple directions at the same time. This is how associations work, after all. Thus, the mind map replicates the exact manner in which our brain learns and memorizes and thus, understanding and translating the ideas on paper becomes an easy task.

Mind mapping is in fact a recommended study tool for students, especially those studying at higher levels of academia. A study conducted in 2010 found that medical students who used mind mapping techniques were able to retain information by a measure of ten percent more than their colleagues who didn't use it.

Mind mapping also helps children recall words better than lists (Buzan and Buzan, 1996). In addition to this, another study discovered that even short-term working memory draw benefits from the chunking process that is inherent to mind mapping, not just long-term memory (Buzan and Buzan, 1996). Last but not least, mind maps are a fun and creative way to engage kids more with a subject thanks to allowing them to visualize and create pictures of their own, as opposed to reading a wall of text on a piece of paper.

So, mind maps are perfect, right? Well, not quite.

## *Drawbacks*

Mind maps of late have been stripped of all nuance and are being presented as a cure-all for all sorts of memorization and learning problems. This is simply not true.

This technique will not benefit those who are extremely logical in nature and like working through things in a linear fashion. Admittedly, there are very few people on this planet who think in this way, but they do exist. If you're one of them, mind maps will actually harm your thinking and creative processes.

The key is to realize that everyone learns differently. For some people, mind maps may result in real lightbulb moments and change their way of thinking and for some, it might bring marginal improvement. Then there are those who might experience reduced creativity and productivity thanks to them. No one is the same, and that's the beauty of our species.

Furthermore, there is a tendency to dismiss linearity as a staid and old-fashioned method of thinking. This is simplifying things to the extent that it simply isn't true. Yes, linearity doesn't help a lot of us at the start of a project, but once a skeleton of a roadmap has been formed, it is linearity that gives us direction.

Put it this way; when a lot of ideas are running around inside your head, pinging off one another, a mind map is your best tool. If you know how the ideas relate to one another and are able to put them in order, a list is your best bet.

As a practical example, let's say you wake up and then realize you have a number of to-do's that day.

You now need to prioritize them and a nice linear list can help you.

The last drawback of mind maps is that they tend to be extremely personal things. What I mean is it's a visual representation of what you have thought of. As such, using a mind map in a group setting could cause some problems, although sometimes it can be a real strength. It all depends on the group members.

Everyone is likely to bring something new to the table. We need a balance between individual and group work. It is necessary to achieve harmony between the points of view, language, experiences, motivations, objectives, tools, emotions, sensitivity, skills and knowledge of the various participants.

Thus, in a group setting, such as defining a project roadmap, it is best to work individually, or in a very small group of no more than three like-minded people and then define a list.

# Aiding Memorization

The first step to creating a mind map is to grab a sheet of paper or a whiteboard. There do exist software which can help you create mind maps for you, but I recommend using them only if you're planning something that doesn't need to be memorized. For memorization purposes, it is best to put pen to paper.

Speaking of pens, you don't need to stick to a regular ink pen. Use crayons, pencils, different colored ink, whatever you can think of. The key is to make the visual impact of the mind map as large as possible. Start off by drawing a circle in the center of the page and writing the gist or name of your idea/problem in the center.

You can give this idea a visual cue which can be anything you can draw. It doesn't have to make sense to anyone but you, remember. So if you're trying to memorize a bunch of historical facts or a family tree, if a compass represents your great grandpa, go for it. Next, brainstorm on the ideas and thoughts that are associated with this central idea.

A number of them will pop up into your head. If you have no idea at all thanks to the topic being completely unfamiliar to you, do some research and reading on it. You don't need to go in depth but just get an idea of what it's about and how it can apply to your audience.

When doing this initially, you will find yourself writing a small summary of the ideas but as you progress, try to jot down just the keywords for each idea as illustrated in the relevant chapter in this book.

Now you'll have around four or five ideas which are associated with the central topic. Some of these ideas will be more relevant to your audience or you than others. Connect these ideas to the central idea with a thick line or anything else that signifies a strong connection. You could give the associated idea a strong and bold outline.

Now, explore that connected idea more. Most likely there will be offshoots of that associated idea and give them the same treatment as you did the main associated ideas. Give them their own little thought clouds and linkages according to their importance and relevance.

In this manner, explore all the associated ideas in your drawing and give each of them their offshoots and jot down how they connect to one another.

Make sure to give each linkage a strong visual cue so that you can instantly picture what's going on with that relationship with just a glance. Use colors to enhance this effect.

Lastly, look for any cross connections between ideas. Most likely there will be some overlap between topics. Join them appropriately either by sharing a cloud or by drawing a link between the relevant clouds. Review your drawing and make any changes you wish.

This final picture is your mind map and is a radial collection of all your ideas on the topic. Pretty isn't it? Well, the objective isn't to beautify the thing, the idea is to be able to visually imprint this picture into your head. The first few times, you'll struggle with some of the details. With practice though, you'll soon be able to memorize entire batches of ideas and will be able to instantly refer to your mind map to figure out where they fits in the scheme of things. In effect, your mind map is really the neural network you are creating within your brain.

## Tips and Tricks

Mind maps are a great tool if used well, but the danger always lies in people thinking they aren't creative enough to draw stuff on paper. This is because of a mistaken belief that mind maps need to be pretty. Look, you're not trying to usurp Raffaello's position in the artistic pantheon here. No one cares if your drawing is bad.

Your mind map is yours and keep it that way. Create whatever makes sense to you and don't give up on it until you've done it a few times. You'll find that repetition, in this case, will aid you greatly and the quality of what you produce will shock you as you progress.

Another good idea is to create your mind maps in environments that inspire you or bring you calm and peace. So for example, if you're taking a walk along the beach at sunset, or up in the hills or anywhere in nature, why not carry along a notepad and a pencil? Doodle when you have the time. Being in nature, calms your mind and makes it more receptive to ideas and memories. Remember that this is a creative process. You don't know by what logic your creative mechanism works, or if there even is one. All you need to know is that it is there and it is there solely to help you. So get out of its way and let it do its thing.

You'll often find that when you create mind maps, if you free yourself enough, you'll end up with another circle which supplants your original circle as the central idea. This is a good thing. It might not make sense to you at the moment and might seem ridiculous, but I guarantee that upon further exploration, it will make sense to you. These things don't happen by accident and you'll find yourself stumbling upon great ideas in this manner.

Remember to use visual cues that are as striking as possible. A good idea is to use the principles of the ridiculous method as outlined earlier.

Make imagery that is as ridiculous as possible. Perhaps you try to draw an elephant that ends up looking like a turnip? Great! Elephant-turnip is your visual cue! There's no way you're going to forget that, once you've stopped laughing at yourself.

Use colors and shades to highlight your ideas but don't try to create a painting. That's not the idea here. Make it striking, but once you find some emotional impact in it, move on. Experiment with the shapes of the thought clouds, perhaps giving the more important ones a circular shape and the lesser ones a square shape and so on.

Last but not least, eliminate every form of distraction when you're doing this. No emails, no messages, no phone calls, no internet and so on. Just you, your thoughts and paper.

As I mentioned earlier, there are excellent software out there which will help you create mind maps. When used as a teaching tool and collaborative tool, these are excellent, but when developing personal ideas, it's best to use pen(cil) and paper. The idea is to personalize it as much as possible and nothing is more personal than something you create by hand.

# 8. Tapping into the Subconscious Mind

Our brains are incredibly complex things. On one hand, they can be divided into biological sections, such as the amygdala, prefrontal cortex and so on; and on the other, it can also be divided on the basis of the functions each portion of the brain plays.

Finally, our brain can also be classified on the basis of thoughts. What I mean by this is, irrespective of the origin of the thought, our brain has multiple levels at which it functions. Popularly, we refer to these levels as the conscious mind, subconscious, and sometimes a third category, the unconscious mind.

Looking at the task of boosting memory through the prism of the subconscious mind might be a bit confusing. This chapter will open your eyes, and mind, to the power that the subconscious and unconscious mind have and how your memory can be significantly boosted through the right methods.

But first, we need to dive deep and understand the nature of our minds.

## Mind and Brain

Mind and brain are often mistakenly used interchangeably. I'd like to make a definite distinction between the terms. The brain refers to the biological organ, and in this chapter, any biological function will be referred to using this term. For example, if talking about which areas are stimulated when laughing, I'll refer to it as areas of the brain.

The mind is a more complex thing and there is the possibility of veering onto a spiritual path. Such a digression is unavoidable and I promise to keep this to a minimum. The mind simply refers to the set of cognitive activities of every living being. It also includes that collection of thoughts you possess and ones which raise their heads during certain situations. Thoughts which block your thinking or weigh you down are also a part of the mind.

When talking of the subconscious, unconscious and conscious mind, we're talking about the mind and not the brain. The mind is a vast topic and governs pretty much everything in your life, via your mindset.

The mindset is a set of ideas, convictions, opinions and mental representations; it is a particular way of conceiving, understanding, feeling and judging reality.

According to my studies of primordial psychology, mentality is something extremely connected to the perception of reality. Is a collection of beliefs and neural networks in the brain, which activates in certain situations. Once the trigger for a situation is activated, via sensory information, the corresponding neural network in our brains are activated. This gives rise to certain thoughts that causes us to act the way we think.

## *Conscious Mind*

The conscious mind includes those processes that we are aware of such as thought, intuition, reason, memory and will.

Right now, as you're reading this book, you're aware of the words you're reading and their meaning. You are also forming your own thoughts in response to these words and can modify and control these thoughts to a certain extent.

This portion of your mind comprises just five percent of your overall thoughts despite occupying such a large percentage of your consciousness. Sigmund Freud referred to the conscious mind as the tip of the iceberg, the bit that peeks out above the water.

The conscious mind is perhaps the smartest portion of the mind and has the power of logic and reasoning. It has the ability to reject and form ideas. The conscious mind does have some creative ability, but this is not its primary function. In a word, its function could be defined as rationality. In any situation, no matter how emotionally charged, we have the power to focus our conscious mind down rational paths and devise solutions.

Given its rational bent, the conscious mind is quite hampered when it comes to creative projects. This does not mean that artists and those in artistic fields have smaller conscious minds, far from it. It's just that much of their work is not produced from the conscious mind.

In fact, almost every single person functions the same way when it comes to carrying out tasks. For example, when a baseball batter needs to hit the ball, he doesn't stop to think and analyze the speed or curve of the ball. Neither does he bust out his protractor and try to measure the dip of the ball and the angle at which the pitcher releases the shot. Instead, he simply uses his eyes and reacts.

This brings up an excellent point, the conscious mind is the first stop when it comes to learning anything. When the batter first picked up a bat, he had nowhere near the skill level he now possesses as a major league professional. He paid attention to his every single movement, he had to learn to identify the pitcher's movements, the ball and so on.

The important point to note here is that his conscious mind did not store anything within itself. It simply passed on the information and effectively forgot about it. The next time it saw a pitch that it had learned previously, it received the learned memory from somewhere else and only identified the possible hit of the ball. Once this was done, it stepped out of the way.

So where was it passing on its information?

## Subconscious Mind

Going back to Dr. Freud's iceberg analogy, the conscious mind was simply passing the information underwater, to the remaining ninety-five percent of the batter's mind. This remaining percentage comprises of the subconscious mind and is responsible for the overwhelming majority of our thoughts and actions.

When it comes to learning techniques, of which memorization is a part of, the subconscious mind is the most important part of it all. Much like how working memory transfers thoughts into long-term memory, the conscious mind does the same and transfers lessons learned into the subconscious mind.

Does this mean the conscious mind is the same as working memory? Well, not exactly. While working memory refers to just things remembered or retained, the conscious mind and the subconscious mind encapsulates behaviors which govern whether or not the memory will be stored in the first place. For example, if a particular lesson triggers a painful emotional reaction, your subconscious mind will inform your conscious mind of this and you simply will not memorize the lesson.

Going back to our example of the baseball player; if he was hit painfully in the face, or anywhere else by the ball, he's unlikely to learn how to identify cues since his subconscious mind will simply not let him learn the lesson or even not allow him to swing the bat because it will convey messages of fear to the conscious mind and he will probably just freeze.

The subconscious mind thus plays a huge role in determining our ability to memorize and learn things. What makes things complicated is that we do not have direct access to our subconscious mind. We're simply not aware of what's in there. We can consciously think of ourselves as excellent dancers but if your subconscious thinks you are bad, you will bad at it, no matter how much you try to learn or the quality of your teacher. I hope you can see where I'm going with this.

You should always keep in mind this Henry Ford quote:

*"Whether you think you can, or you think you can't, you're right."*

The subconscious is where our beliefs are stored and if you try to approach memory improvement with a belief that your memory is bad, no amount of techniques are going to help you. This is what I've been emphasizing throughout this book that there is no such thing as a poor memory. You, like every human being on this planet, have the ability to remember everything you want. It's just that you're untrained, not bad at it.

This is also why I've been emphasizing memory as a skill and not as a personal quality or trait. A skill can be learned and improved upon. A personality trait is a far more nebulous thing. How does one become less impulsive, for example? Contrast this with someone coming up to you and asking you how he could go about improving their reading abilities. For the latter, we can provide a definite path, whereas the former would be a maze of ideas.

If you think of memory improvement as an inherited or genetic trait this is probably because you haven't experienced how much your memory can improve with a few simple exercises. That's why the second book in this series has been dedicated to memory and brain training. And that's also why I've included some memory exercises and games in this book. Once you do these you'll gain the experience of having your memory boosted via some simple techniques.

Once this happens, your belief that is wired into your brain and produces the subconscious thought in your mind, the one regarding your inability to improve your memory, weakens just that little bit. This is where repetition comes in. Repeatedly hammering home the message that you can improve your memory since it's a skill will build another neural network and simply deactivate the old one. The way to do this is to keep practicing the memory building exercises in this book and the other two books in this series.

Your inherent beliefs are why you might not have seen any improvement in your memory skills if you've tried all sorts of games and tricks in the past. Or, as is far more common, you might have seen improvement but then simply stopped working on it and experienced a regression. Perhaps you got lazy or didn't feel like continuing with it. Why do you think this happened?

It was simply your subconscious mind asserting the old beliefs over the new ones, and the brain exerting the old neural network in place of the new one and thus, you went back to your old rhythms. As long as that belief is present within your subconscious mind, you're not going to see lasting improvement. Here's a simple test: With the exercises I've shown you in this book and techniques, such as chunking, linking, pegging etc., it is fully possible for you to walk into a room full of people, say a hundred, and memorize all of their first and last names and then recount it to everybody at the end of the evening.

Think this is impossible? Does it sound improbable? Well, let's try this instead: By continuous practice and correct training and discipline and a little talent, it is possible for a boy to eventually play in the major leagues. This statement doesn't sound improbable, does it? Yet, the previous one does. Why should it? I'm talking about the same thing, which is the development of skill. What are your beliefs regarding memory improvement in light of these statements?

As you read those statements, a small voice within your head probably whispered, "it's possible for people, but not me." This is an interesting little subset of your subconscious mind we will now look at.

## *Unconscious Mind*

The unconscious mind is an extremely interesting thing. Opinion is divided as to whether it exists as a separate entity or is a full subset of the subconscious mind (Hanson and Mendius, 2009). The exact nature of this does not concern us. Instead, we're more concerned with the functions of this portion of our mind.

The unconscious mind is that part of us that has recorded all the data, not immediately available to consciousness, but stored up to form a collection of our beliefs about ourselves, which determine much of who we are.

Who are we? What are we like? What is "I"? If the subconscious mind determines everything that happens in our reality, then unconscious determines a lot of beliefs that exist within the subconscious mind.

Our identities and self-images are formed at a very young age and unless we experience traumatic conditions later in life or a significant brain injury, they pretty much stay in place (Hanson and Mendius, 2009). This is not to say that our self-images never change. There is additional nuance added to it as we grow older and understand things better. However, the deep underpinnings of our personalities are formed before the age of seven and it is through this prism we view everything around us.

Thus, if you grew up in an environment which valued academics over sports, you'll end up believing that sports as a career can never amount to anything serious. In order to support this image of yourself, you will develop additional beliefs within your subconscious. Beliefs such as a baseball being capable of causing life-altering damage to your face. Your actions will be in line with this belief and guess what happens? You wear a baseball right on your nose; this reinforces the belief.

Our perception of reality shapes our beliefs. These beliefs shape our actions and our actions determine our results. Our beliefs are shaped by our self-images. This is why it isn't enough to simply change a few surface level beliefs to bring about lasting change. You need to dig deep and actually change your own self-image of who you are.

This is what I do mainly, I empower people's minds through mental reprogramming. Most mental reprogramming programs fail because they overshadow the crucial role that mental empowerment plays. But fortunately this is what I specialize in. I help people empower their minds in the shortest possible time.

I have been studying the mind since 2003 and over the years I have created a protocol with powerful strategies, advanced methods and new ways of thinking and acting, to increase the ability to achieve personal and professional goals and to elevate performance to extraordinary levels.

I have called it **"The Zeloni Magelli Protocol"** and year after year it is becoming the European reference path for mental strengthening. And the thing that gratifies me most of all is not only the recognition of some colleagues and trainers, but the certificates of esteem that I receive daily from my students.

Going back to your memory, if you think of yourself as someone who doesn't have a good memory or is forgetful, you need not bother changing the surface beliefs that result from this self-image. Instead, attacking the root cause which is your identity will deactivate a whole host of dependent beliefs. This is both a good and a bad thing.

The good thing is that you don't need to scan your whole mind looking for every single belief in your head. You just need to focus on one thing. You can develop an extraordinary memory. The bad news is that if you are convinced that memory is not a skill, perhaps points to a bigger problem within you.

If this belief is very strong, it will take time to root out it and you will need patience and a lot of repetition along with emotions.

A lot of people believe that talent is somehow essential to succeed. This is simply not true. More than anything else, it is hard work that determines success. In her book, *Mindset*, Dr. Carol Dweck describes in great detail about how talented individuals eventually fall short to those who work hard (Dweck, 2012).

Talent does determine marginal cases. For example, the phenomenon, the footballer Ronaldo Luís Nazário de Lima, even when he trained little and was out of shape, still made a difference. Or, you can work as hard as you can, more than anyone else in the world, but in the Olympic 100m men's finals, you're unlikely to run faster than Usain Bolt in his prime, who was a once in a lifetime genetic freak, possessing a large frame which gave him a longer stride and the explosive ability of someone much shorter.

Some people are just luckier than others, there's no denying that. However, this does not mean that you can run for the Olympics. Hard work will always win out over someone who is talented but doesn't work as much. This is much evident when you listen to any successful person (Dweck, 2012).

Read these words of a famous commercial carefully. This is Michael Jordan's monologue:

*"Maybe it's my own fault. Maybe I led you to believe it was easy when it wasn't.*

*Maybe I made you think my highlights started at the free throw line, and not in the gym.*

*Maybe I made you think that every shot I took was a game winner. That my game was built on flash, and not fire.*

*Maybe it's my fault that you didn't see that failure gave me strength; that my pain was my motivation.*

*Maybe I led you to believe that basketball was a God given gift, and not something I worked for every single day of my life.*

*Maybe I destroyed the game. Or maybe you're just making excuses."*

Also think about these words by Michelangelo Buonarroti:

*"If people knew how hard I had to work to gain my mastery, it would not seem so wonderful at all."*

The reason I'm mentioning all this is to convince you of the fact that memory is a skill that can be learned and there's no such thing as being born with a talent for remembering things. Now, someone may have a marginal talent in this area, but that hardly matters. Unless you've had a significant brain injury, the difference is negligible. With work, you too can possess excellent memorization skills.

Thus, you can see how the subconscious mind does play an important role in determining your ability to believe in your ability to remember things. In other words, it is the foundation of your palace while your memorization skills are a room within, one among many.

Ensure your foundation is strong and everything else will fall in line. So how do you train and strengthen your subconscious mind?

## Training the Subconscious

Training the subconscious requires you to apply the principles of learning we looked at in the first chapter: emotions, repetition and intention. There is focus as well but these three together determine your level of focus so it gets taken care of along the way.

There are a variety of methods ranging from hypnosis to affirmations in order to train your subconscious, here I will share some powerful techniques that will work.

## *Meditation*

This first technique is probably the best. Meditation has been around forever and since ancient times has been prescribed as the best exercise for the brain. It is an ancient and universal practice fundamental to increase one's performance at every level, both mental and physical.

By now, numerous studies have confirmed how this inner process reestablishes the brain's ability at various levels to bring you a feeling of great balance and well-being. Not only does meditation strengthen the mind, but it also calms it down radically and your ability to classify things in the right order of importance will increase dramatically (Hanson and Mendius, 2009).

Meditation literally changes your brain. By practicing it, you will be rewiring your neural networks since what you're actually doing is changing your thought patterns. There are many forms of meditation, all the way from observing your breath to increasing your body's core temperature

(Foreman, 2015). You don't need to become a monk in order to meditate. It is best approached in a step-by-step way.

If you are approaching the topic for the first time, it may seem difficult, but it is not. You need to start finding a comfortable and spontaneous position, in order to reach a nice level of relaxation and abandonment. There is no more or less right position, there is the right position for you!

It can help you create a mental garden where you can take refuge to find absolute peace and tranquility, a state of intense relaxation and well-being that allows you to increase your energy.

Don't think about what you do, close your eyes, relax your arms, your body, concentrate on your breathing and let yourself go. Lower your mind control, slow down all your processes, alternating between concentration and distraction phases to listen to the conversations of your silence. You will notice that your thoughts come and go freely n and out of your head and you will feel a nice feeling of calm and order. You will feel very relaxed.

Meditating restores balance and harmony to the functioning of your brain and your mood thanks to dopamine and serotonin. It helps you to calm down effectively so you can focus on your priorities and make the most of your brain. It also helps you let go of everything that weighs you down, that slows you down, that hinders your true being.

Of course this is just a brief introduction to meditation. Once you have done some basic exercise, you should pick a particular practice of meditation and follow it.

The most followed practices are those of Samatha and Vipassana. While the core objectives of both are different and their techniques differ, really, there's no huge benefit of one over the other. Just pick one and start learning it, preferably from a qualified teacher. The latter technique builds your focus, but this doesn't mean Vipassana will harm it or not build it, so don't worry about their specific aims. Start with one, but then try to learn as many disciplines as possible to complete and consolidate your mental and personal growth.

There are religious forms of meditation as well and if you feel comfortable with them, feel free to go ahead with it. Again, the point is to exercise and control your mind and thus, rewire your beliefs. This goes far beyond just memory improvement as you can imagine.

## *Visualization*

I've already touched upon the huge benefits of visualization previously. Our brain cannot tell the difference between imagined and real thoughts. Therefore, why not use this to your advantage to change your beliefs?

Why not visualize yourself standing in front of people, dazzling them with your memory abilities? Imagine yourself recalling everyone's name and remembering their names despite meeting them just once and then seeing them again after a few years. Your self-image plays a big role in this process as does emotion.

The effect of emotion is pretty easy to understand at this point. By focusing on how good such feats of memory, you'll give your brain further incentive to embed these pictures down into your long-term memory and thus influence your self-image. However, your self-image is not going to sit back and take it lightly.

If your images are grandiose right from that start, you can certainly expect that voice in the back of your head to pipe up and say "this is BS". It will convince you that all this visualization stuff is just spiritual hokum and you're better off the way you are. Aren't you already comfortable? So why change anything?

This is, of course, your mind expressing itself thanks to old neural networks being activated in your brain. The solution to all this is to simply take small bites at the apple. So don't start off with the image of you dazzling everyone, but begin with yourself successfully carrying out your practice tasks and seeing improvement. It doesn't have to be a huge improvement, just a small one is good enough.

This is a believable picture for your self-image and in this manner, you can change your thoughts. By slowly increasing the degree of your feats in your mental pictures and accompanying them with strong positive emotion, you will eventually change your beliefs about yourself.

You have to understand that the first ability to create anything is the ability of imagination. In fact, people who achieve extraordinary successes have the great skill of being able to visualize. They have the ability to create exciting images of themselves and their future.

It has been shown that if you can't see a certain future scenario in your mind, it will be very difficult for you to be able to realize it. If you think about it, all the great feats, great inventions and great innovations in history were first born in someone's mind. They originated from a mental image of some person.

For example, the great geniuses of the past had the ability to think big and created their inventions first in their mind and then in reality. They managed to turn into reality what for many people were impossible dreams, simply because they had imagined them before.

Think, what you have achieved in your life, you had achieved first in your mind, everything is first thought and then realized. First you make the project, and then the construction, first you conceive the image and then you take actions to transform the image into reality.

This is one of the secrets of the world's greatest men and women. Become the person you imagine you are. Learning to use your imagination to create images of your future and then manage them allows you to become the creator of your own destiny.

Read carefully, several times, these words of Jack Nicklaus. He is widely considered to be one of the greatest golfers of all time.

*"I never hit a shot, even in practice, without having a very sharp, in-focus picture of it in my head. It's like a color movie. First I 'see' the ball where I want*

*it to finish, nice and white and setting up high on the bright green grass. Then the scene quickly changes and I 'see' the ball going there; its path, trajectory, and shape, even its behavior on landing. Then there's a sort of a fade-out, and the next scene shows me making the kind of swing that will turn in the images into reality."*

I don't want to convey the message that just visualization is enough to make things happen and achieve the desired changes in life. Because you have to work a lot on yourself, remember the words of Michelangelo and Michael Jordan. But visualization is very important to achieve our goals.

Eliminate your mental images of failure and replace them with successful mental images. You will change your mood to face your challenges. Your mental clarity will be different and you will access different resources. You'll behave differently and achieve your goals more effectively.

## *Affirmations*

Affirmations are just positive self talk. Unfortunately for many people, they are required because they tend to indulge in extremely negative self talk. A lot of this arises from their subconscious and unconscious mind. A poor self-image leads to a lot of damaging self talk and translates into a miserable existence.

Affirmations, whether positive or negative, are thus a function of your self-image. This is why a lot of them don't work for people. It isn't enough to simply repeat to yourself a number of positive messages. If your self-image feels they're false, you'll internally reject them, much like you would reject grandiose images (Hanson and Mendius, 2009).

So when it comes to positive self talk, you need to implement the bite-sized approach along with another crucial element. Your statements need to be in the present tense and written as if you've already achieved them. Much like how your mental imagery convinces your brain that everything you're visualizing is actually happening or has happened, writing things in the present tense helps to convince your brain that your outcome is real.

Thus, make sure to scale your statements up. How do you determine where to start? Well, this is where meditation comes in handy. Meditation will give you a keen awareness as to which thoughts are floating through your mind and when reciting your statements, if you feel some sort of negative pushback or feeling that it isn't true or is rubbish, you need to dial things down a bit.

Rather depressingly, in some instances, you might need to dial it down all the way to zero. Which is to say that your statements will take the form of celebrating the absence of a negative as opposed to the presence of a positive. This is perfectly fine. Again, just like mind maps, this is a personal thing so don't sweat it.

Combining these three techniques will give you massive results with regard to changing your beliefs and putting your brain in a better situation so as to aid your memorization abilities. It will take work and patience but over time, with discipline, you'll see some real changes in your ability to carry out whatever task you wish.

The subconscious mind is extremely powerful and the good thing is that you can control it perfectly. It doesn't have the ability to reject what you give it and thus, make sure you only feed it positive mental imagery and statements.

This concludes our look at how you can utilize your subconscious mind's power to improve your brain's overall health and engage your creative faculties better. A lot of this will take time but you'll be surprised by how soon you manage to get things going with steady practice. The key to all this, as always, is repetition.

If you want really effective help to empower your mind and achieve the goals you want, remember the Zeloni Magelli Protocol. I will empower your mind in the shortest possible time.

# A Better Memory, A Better You

So here we are at the end. Along the way, you've learned of biological facts and practice techniques, along with some out of left field techniques which will boost not just your memory skills but also your brain's overall health. In addition to the techniques, exercises and games detailed in the other two books in this series, you should have a full picture of how memory, learning and the brain's biological processes tie together.

Always remember the keys to learning, which are focus, repetition, intentionality and emotion. Focus is something that arises out of implementing the other three. While you can practice standalone focus exercises, the best way to develop focus is to let it come to you naturally. That is, if you're interested in what you're doing, you'll focus by yourself. It is things you're not interested in that make it difficult for you to focus on. Another reason, people find it hard to focus on things they love doing is because their brains are tired and need rest. Many people tend to take mental health and well-being with less seriousness than it warrants and this is a shame.

My point is, this is where intentionality comes in. I've talked quite a bit about emotion and repetition, the latter being quite obvious, but intentionality is a more nebulous concept and you would think, justifiably, that intentionality should come under the focus umbrella. Well, in this context intentionality refers to your lifestyle goals and prioritization.

What is the intention behind a lot of the tasks you choose to do? You probably go to work every day and put up with a lot of stress that results from it. What is your intention behind doing all this? Do you even know? You might have taken up your job with some intentions in mind, but are that still valid now?

These are important questions because many people find themselves exchanging the purpose for the medium. They would like to realize themselves with a job, improve their health, have more free time, more money and better relationships. But as a result of a paradox most of them find themselves without time, without money, with a lot of stress and in solitude.

Stop and think. Is what you're doing pushing you away or getting closer to your goals? These are important questions that need to be evaluated in order to reward the risk. Every action you perform places a cognitive load on your brain and could cause stress if you don't do what you like. If you're undertaking that stress for a good reason, it is justifiable, but adding stress for no valid reason is a surefire way to a miserable life. Simply put, you'll be too tired to do anything else, since such activities place a higher energy demand on you.

For example, raising a child may be one of the most stressful things you'll do in your life. However, almost every parent will agree that the stress was worth it. Will people say the same thing about their jobs? Unlikely. You see, lifestyle factors go beyond just what you're doing right now. You need to look at what you will be doing down the line as well.

Remember that your brain is only going to deteriorate and not get younger or magically healthier if you do nothing. As mentioned earlier, everything that I've spoken about in these three books works to keep your brain's health better. Ultimately, none of us stand a chance against time. Although there are many skills that can be improved up to 70 years and on many fields the more you grow and the better you improve, see the experience.

Thus, it is of the greatest importance that you prioritize your brain's health and wellbeing and regard stress and negativity (which causes a lot of unwanted stress through fear), as mortal enemies. It is vital that you use as many aids as possible to help your overall health along with that of your brain. Make it your intention to do things that are as kind to you as possible and have a greater reward than the stress you undertake to complete them.

Don't misunderstand this sentence. I'm not telling you to live a risk-free life, otherwise there would be no growth. Facing new challenges is good for the brain, and great rewards lie behind great challenges.

Everything I've given you thus far will do this and more. There are two additional ways for you to reinforce information and learn better. These are by using music and writing. Music, generates more emotion than pretty much everything else in this world.

There's a lot of talk about what sort of music is best for the human brain and a lot of it goes back to brain wave theories. Baroque classical music has been said to stimulate alpha waves within the brain and aid in learning and expanding the brain's neural networks. Now, as with a lot of brain wave based memory improvement techniques, credible research is close to nonexistent with these theories (Ball, 2011).

There are currently many types of music sold commercially that are branded as "relaxation aids." However, the claims that the music can induce psychological and physical relaxation are rarely validated on an empirical basis (Lee-Harris et al., 2018).

For example, you often hear about meditative music or binaural beats, but do these sounds work better than classical music? That depends. Meditative music and binaural beats may effectively contribute to relaxation, but in a way that differs depending on age (Lee-Harris et al., 2018).

What I'm trying to tell you is that there is no science that shows that one music is better than another. Instead of worrying about what sort of music is best, why not just focus on the type of emotion the music creates within you. We listen to different types of music for different reasons. Sometimes, we listen to certain tracks when we're down and need a boost; sometimes we listen to a particular set when we're happy and want to rejoice. Then there's the stuff that lulls us to sleep at night.

Instead of focusing on the genre of music focus on the emotion it raises within you. Now, tracks that make you feel better when you're low might seem a good choice, but over the long run, this sort of music listening only reinforces that things are bad. If you find yourself listening to music in this manner most of the time, the fault is not with the music but it is merely a symptom that something needs to be fixed in your life.

The best sort of music to listen to is one which helps you rejoice and puts you in an upbeat mood. You'll find that such music will be listened to by most people when they're already in a good mood. Thus, the goal or intention here is not to use music in some magical way, but to simply strive to feel good most of the time.

Feel good doesn't mean you reject emotions of sadness or anxiety. These occur naturally and there's a very good reason for them so do not make the mistake of invalidating them. However, strive to make things as good as possible. If you're sad, don't aim to reject the sadness and start jumping for joy. Instead, aim to make the sadness feel less bad and climb the ladder back to neutral and then happy.

Small bites, remember?

You could use music as an aid to memory as detailed in the previous books in this series as a mnemonic device. However, remember to use the transformative power of music to your favor.

Writing is another great tool. Think of writing as a drain for your negative emotions and simply unload them out on paper. Don't censor yourself or put a stopper to the flow of thoughts once you get going. However, just like with music, if you find that you're using writing in this manner most of the time, something's wrong that you need to fix and your intentionality isn't pointed in the favor of living well and being kind to yourself.

The memory is very important, if we cannot memorize our experiences, emotions, people, words and numbers, we will not be able to think. Remembering is an art that can be learned by anyone. Everyone can develop their individual memory.

The human brain is an extremely powerful machine

and there is still much to discover. What we do know is that it is more powerful than we know and we need to stop sabotaging its efforts by placing our everyday, mundane worries upon it.

So the way forward, and your targeted intention is clear: Be kind to yourself. Prioritize your well-being. Everything else, including super memory, will follow.

**UPGRADE YOUR MIND** -> zelonimagelli.com

**UPGRADE YOUR BUSINESS** -> zeloni.eu

EDOARDO ZELONI MAGELLI

# PHOTOGRAPHIC MEM RY

Basic and Advanced Memory
Techniques to Improve Your Memory
-
Mnemonic Techniques and Strategies
to Enhance Memorization

EDOARDO
ZELONI MAGELLI

EDOARDO ZELONI MAGELLI

# MEMRY TRAINING

Memory Games and Brain Training to Improve Memory and Prevent Memory Loss
-
Mental Training for Enhancing Memory and Concentration and Sharpening Cognitive Function

EDOARDO
ZELONI MAGELLI

# Bibliographical References

Adegbuyi, F. (2019). *Deep Work: The Complete Guide (including a step-by-step checklist)*. [online] Ambition & Balance. Retrieved July 7, 2019, from https://doist.com/blog/complete-guide-to-deep-work/

Alharbi, Mudi H. and Lamport, Daniel J. and Dodd, Georgina F. and Saunders, Caroline and Harkness, Laura and Butler, Laurie T. and Spencer, Jeremy P. E. (2016). Flavonoid-rich orange juice is associated with acute improvements in cognitive function in healthy middle-aged males. *European Journal of Nutrition*, 55 (6). pp. 2021-2029. ISSN 1436-6215

American Addiction Centers. (2019). *Depression, Anger, and Addiction: The Role of Emotions in Recovery and Treatment*. Retrieved July 7, 2019, from https://americanaddictioncenters.org/co-occurring-disorders/emotions-in-recovery-and-treatment

Ball, P. (2011). *The music instinct*. London: Vintage Books.

Bryant, J. (2016) *An Investment In Knowledge Pays The Best Interest.* Retrieved April 14, 2020, from https://selfmadesuccess.com/about-justin-bryant/

Buzan, T. and Buzan, B. (1996). *The mind map book*.

New York: Plume.

Debono M, Ghobadi C, Rostami-Hodjegan A, Huatan H, Campbell MJ, Newell-Price J, Darzy K, Merke DP, Arlt W, & Ross RJ (2009). Modified-release hydrocortisone to provide circadian cortisol profiles. *The Journal of clinical endocrinology and metabolism,* 94 (5), 1548-54.

Dweck, C. (2012). *Mindset.* [Kennett Square, PA]: Soundview Executive Book Summaries.

Farnam Street. (2019). *The Buffett Formula: Going to Bed Smarter Than When You Woke Up.* Retrieved July 7, 2019, from https://fs.blog/2013/05/the-buffett-formula/

Foreman, C. (2015). *Revealing the Secrets of Tibetan Inner Fire Meditation* Retrieved July 7, 2019, from https://www.thewayofmeditation.com.au/revealing-the-secrets-of-tibetan-inner-fire-meditation

Grant, A. (2016). *Originals.* 1st ed. [S.l.]: Penguin Publishing Group.

Hanson, R. and Mendius, R. (2009). *Buddha's brain.* Oakland, CA: New Harbinger Publications.

Human-memory.net. (2019). *Memory Encoding - Memory Processes - The Human Memory.* Retrieved July 7, 2019, from http://www.human-memory.net/processes_encoding.html

Ifc.unam.mx. (2019). *A Brief Introduction to the Brain:*

*Themes*. Retrieved July 7, 2019, from http://www.ifc.unam.mx/Brain/segunda.htm

Ifc.unam.mx. (2019). *A Brief Introduction to the Brain: Neural Nets*. Retrieved July 7, 2019, from http://www.ifc.unam.mx/Brain/nenet.htm

Jennings, K. (2017). *11 Best Foods to Boost Your Brain and Memory*. Healthline. Retrieved July 7, 2019, from https://www.healthline.com/nutrition/11-brain-foods#section1

Kubala, J. (2019). *6 Ways Added Sugar Is Fattening*. Healthline. Retrieved July 7, 2019, from https://www.healthline.com/nutrition/does-sugar-make-you-fat

Lee-Harris, G. Timmers, R. Humberstone, N. Blackburn, D. (2008) Music for Relaxation: A Comparison Across Two Age Groups. *Journal of Music Therapy*, Volume 55, Issue 4, Winter 2018, Pages 439–462.

Lucarelli, G. (2015) *La verità, vi prego, su emisfero destro, emisfero sinistro e creatività.* Retrieved July 7, 2019, from http://www.giovannilucarelli.it/wordpress/2015/06/verita-emisfero-destro-emisfero-sinistro/

Musial, C., Kuban-Jankowska, A., Gorska-Ponikowska, M. (2020). Beneficial Properties of Green Tea Catechins. *International Journal of Molecular Sciences* 21(5):1744 March 2020.

Newport, C. (2016). *Deep work*. 1st ed. Little Brown book Group.

Newsonen, S. (2014). *Why Do You Find It so Hard to Not Multitask?*. Psychology Today. Retrieved July 7, 2019, from https://www.psychologytoday.com/intl/blog/the-path-passionate-happiness/201405/why-do-you-find-it-so-hard-not-multitask

Novella, S. (2017). *Brain Wave Pseudoscience*. [online] Sciencebasedmedicine.org. Retrieved July 7, 2019, from https://sciencebasedmedicine.org/brain-wave-pseudoscience/

TalentSmart. (2019). *Emotional Intelligence (EQ) | The Premier Provider - Tests, Training, Certification, and Coaching.* TalentSmart. Retrieved July 7, 2019, from https://www.talentsmart.com/articles/Multitasking-Damages-Your-Brain-and-Your-Career,-New-Studies-Suggest-2102500909-p-1.html

Wax, D. (2019). *Writing and Remembering: Why We Remember What We Write*. Lifehack. Retrieved July 7, 2019, from: https://www.lifehack.org/articles/featured/writing-and-remembering-why-we-remember-what-we-write.html

Xiaochen Lin, Isabel Zhang, Alina Li, JoAnn E Manson, Howard D Sesso, Lu Wang, Simin Liu (2016). Cocoa Flavanol Intake and Biomarkers for Cardiometabolic Health: A Systematic Review and Meta-Analysis of

Randomized Controlled Trials. *The Journal of Nutrition,* Volume 146, Issue 11, November 2016, Pages 2325–2333.

Zamora-Ros R, Forouhi NG, Sharp SJ, González CA, Buijsse B, Guevara M, van der Schouw YT, Amiano P, Boeing H, Bredsdorff L, Clavel-Chapelon F, Fagherazzi G, Feskens EJ, Franks PW, Grioni S, Katzke V, Key TJ, Khaw KT, Kühn T, Masala G, Mattiello A, Molina-Montes E, Nilsson PM, Overvad K, Perquier F, Quirós JR, Romieu I, Sacerdote C, Scalbert A, Schulze M, Slimani N, Spijkerman AM, Tjonneland A, Tormo MJ, Tumino R, van der A DL, Langenberg C, Riboli E, Wareham NJ. (2013). *The association between dietary flavonoid and lignan intakes and incident type 2 diabetes in European populations: the EPIC-InterAct study. Diabetes Care. 2013 Dec;36(12):3961-70. doi: 10.2337/dc13-0877. Epub 2013 Oct 15.*

www.ingramcontent.com/pod-product-compliance
Lightning Source LLC
Chambersburg PA
CBHW072154100526
44589CB00015B/2232